Controlling your Financial Future

How to Increase Your Wealth, Decrease Your Debt, and Manage Your Cash Flow™

A step-by-step program to help you control your financial future with greater confidence, knowledge and peace of mind.

by Betty Meredith, CFA, CFP, CRC

Discover Learning®

Financial education...simply well designed.

Controlling Your Financial Future:
How to Increase Your Wealth,
Decrease Your Debt and
Manage Your Cash Flow™

Second Edition
2nd Printing, 2005

By Betty Meredith, CFA®, CFP®, CRC®
Discover Learning, Inc.

CREDITS:

Editor:	Betty Meredith, CFA, CFP, CRC
Contributing writers:	Susan Blauvelt, Amy L. Whitlatch, CFP®, CDFA
Cover Design:	Chris Shamus, Shamus Design
Typesetting:	Kathy Kull, Sharon Thornton

ISBN 0-9702220-7-6

Discover Learning® books are distributed by Discover Learning, Inc., P.O. Box 130857, Ann Arbor, MI 48113. Telephone: (734) 669-8790 Fax: (734) 669-8792 www.discover-learning.com.

To the Reader:

In November, 1977, my father was killed in an industrial accident. My then 52 year-old mother was left with only a $10,000 whole life insurance policy and mortgage insurance that paid off our modest $30,000 home. We were left without Dad's pension since he was two years short of the fifteen years he needed to be vested. A lack of a basic financial plan unnecessarily undermined our family's financial security, and motivated me to create Discover Learning, Inc. in 1989.

Discover Learning, Inc.'s mission is to enable middle-income employees to experience greater confidence, knowledge and peace of mind when making financial planning decisions so they may enjoy healthier, happier, more productive lives. We believe that all people are capable of creating and following through with a financial plan when they are taught a system to follow and are provided with the proper environment in which to learn. Our materials have also proven to save time and money for those who choose to enlist the help of a financial professional.

Our hands-on, user-friendly, self-study materials and licensable workshops use adult learning methodology to help individuals secure their financial future. Financial education topics include financial planning, 401(k) investing, pre-retirement planning, lump sum distributions, deciding whether to accept an early retirement or voluntary separation offer, and designing and implementing an effective financial education program.

We exist to serve the middle income individuals and families through employers and organizations who value their people, believe in the importance of personal finance, and understand how it affects one's productivity and peace of mind. At Discover Learning, Inc., we truly care about the learner. One hundred percent of our time is spent on designing and delivering effective and enjoyable financial education materials and programs that change lives.

A special thanks to Susan Blauvelt and Amy Whitlatch, CFP, CDFA for their contribution to all of Discover Learning's materials. Your dedication and support have made these books possible. And a special "thank you" to you, the reader, for the privilege to be of service to you.

Best regards,

Betty Meredith, CFA, CFP, CRC
President
Discover Learning, Inc.
Financial education . . . simply well-designed.^{sm}

Table of Contents

INTRODUCTION 1

WELCOME TO *CONTROLLING YOUR FINANCIAL FUTURE* 3
WHY YOU SHOULD ACT NOW TO SECURE YOUR FINANCIAL FUTURE 4
THE PRICE OF PROCRASTINATION 5
THE FINANCIAL PLANNING PROCESS 6
MY ACTION PLAN 7

FIRST BASE: DETERMINE WHERE YOU ARE 9

THE *QUICK CHECK* FINANCIAL ASSESSMENT 10
  The Quick Check Financial Assessment 11
  Review of "NO" Responses to the Quick Check Financial Assessment 14
YOUR NET WORTH ASSESSMENT 19
  Part I: What Is Net Worth? 20
  How the Choices You Make Affect Your Wealth 21
  Part II: Calculating Your Net Worth 22
  Calculating Your Net Worth: Liquid Assets 23
  Calculating Your Net Worth: Loaned Assets 24
  Calculating Your Net Worth: Owned Assets 25
  Calculating Your Net Worth: Personal Assets 26
  Calculating Your Net Worth: Deferred Assets 27
  Calculating Your Net Worth: Liabilities or Money That Is Owed 28
  Net Worth Summary 29
  Part III: Is Your Net Worth As Strong As It Could Be? 30
  Part IV: Average Household Net Worth 31

SECOND BASE: DETERMINE WHERE YOU WANT TO GO 33

VALUES-BASED GOAL SETTING 34
  What is Values-Based Goal Setting? 35
  What's Important to You? 36
  Identifying Possible Goals 37
  List of Potential Goals 38
  Identifying Needs vs. Wants 39
  Your Spending Priorities 40
  In order for goals to be accomplished, they need to be SMART: 41
  So Where Do You Find the Money to Help You Accomplish Your Goals? 42

THIRD BASE: HOW TO CONFIDENTLY ACCOMPLISH YOUR GOALS 43

HOW TO BUILD WEALTH AND CONFIDENTLY ACCOMPLISH YOUR GOALS 45
WEALTH BUILDING: *TAXES AND YOUR RETIREMENT SAVINGS 401(K), 403(B) OR 457 PLANS* 46
REDUCE AND ELIMINATE DEBT 47
  Step I: The Secret to Getting Out of Debt 48
  Step II: Reducing Debt What Do You Owe? 50
  Step III: Reducing Debt 51
  Step IV: Create Your Plan to Reduce and Eliminate Debt 52
INVESTING PRINCIPLE #1: COMPOUNDING 54
  The Risk of Possibly Not Having Enough at Retirement 55
  Setting Goals with Compounding 56
  Chart A - How Much Will My Monthly Savings Be Worth In The Future??? 57
  Chart B - How Much Do I Save Per Month Now If I Want A Certain Dollar Amount In The Future??? 58

Chart C - How Much Will My One-Time Investment Be Worth in the Future?? *59*

Chart D - How Much of a One-Time Investment Do I Put Aside Now to Have a Certain Amount in the Future? *60*

INVESTING PRINCIPLE #2: DIVERSIFICATION *61*

Diversification and Asset Classes *62*

INVESTING PRINCIPLE #3: DOLLAR COST AVERAGING *63*

HOW TO CONFIDENTLY ACCOMPLISH YOUR GOALS SUMMARY *64*

HOME: IMPLEMENT YOUR PLAN **65**

STEP I: WHY USE A SPENDING PLAN (A/K/A A BUDGET)? *66*

STEP II: WHERE IS YOUR MONEY GOING NOW? *68*

Variable Spending Tracking Sheet *69*

Where is Your Money Going Now? *70*

Monthly Fixed Expenses *71*

Monthly Fixed Variable Expenses *72*

Variable Expenses *73*

STEP III: WHERE DO YOU WANT YOUR MONEY TO GO? *74*

Twelve Month Spending Plan *75*

Common Fixed and Periodic Expense Categories *76*

Common Variable Expense Categories *78*

STEP IV: USING YOUR SPENDING PLAN *80*

Average Household Spending: *Fixed Costs* *81*

Average Household Spending: *Variable Costs* *82*

SPENDING PLAN SUMMARY *83*

WORKBOOK SUMMARY *84*

APPENDIX A: ANNUAL UPDATE SYSTEM **85**

MY ACTION PLAN *86*

YOUR ANNUAL CHECKUP SYSTEM *88*

THE *QUICK CHECK* FINANCIAL ASSESSMENT *89*

The Quick Check Financial Assessment *90*

Review of "NO" Responses to the Quick Check Financial Assessment *93*

CHARTING YOUR LEVEL OF DEBT *98*

TRACKING YOUR LEVEL OF DEBT *99*

TRACKING YOUR NET WORTH *100*

NET WORTH SUMMARY *101*

LIST OF POTENTIAL GOALS *102*

IDENTIFYING NEEDS VS. WANTS *103*

IN ORDER FOR GOALS TO BE ACCOMPLISHED, THEY NEED TO BE SMART: *104*

TWELVE MONTH SPENDING PLAN *105*

Variable Spending Tracking Sheet *108*

APPENDIX B: SAMPLE FINANCIAL PLAN **109**

Introduction

Welcome to
CONTROLLING YOUR FINANCIAL FUTURE
How to Increase Your Wealth, Decrease Your
Debt and Manage Your Cash Flow™

Money is one of the most powerful motivators of human behavior. It affects the level of happiness, peace of mind, harmony of relationship within our family, and quality of life we experience over time.

This self-paced, application-oriented workbook is designed to help you establish a more solid financial base so that you may experience a happier, healthier, more productive life.

Workbook Goal:
- To provide you with the knowledge of and process for controlling your financial future with greater confidence and peace of mind.
- To help you create a basic financial plan that you can implement on your own or save you time and money when working with a financial professional.

In "Controlling Your Financial Future"
You Will Learn:
- How you control your financial future by controlling your present money behavior

- How to understand and evaluate your current financial situation and make appropriate changes

- How to set goals, pay down debt and use a spending plan so you will be more financially secure within a year.

As you take control of your financial future, you will notice that you feel like you have more control in other areas of your life, too. Your relationships with your family and co-workers will become more focused, relaxed and productive. You'll find you have more time to spend on activities that are more fulfilling and of higher value to you than worrying about money.

> *Being successful with your money is not a function of how much you have, but rather how well you use it to support your personal values, priorities and needs.*

Why You Should Act Now
to Secure Your Financial Future

Let's explore today's odds of reaching retirement in good financial health. Using a pencil, take a guess at the numbers below. Out of 100 people who would retire today at age 65: (The answers are provided at the bottom of the page.)

- _____ is rich

- _____ are financially independent

- _____ are working to supplement their income

- _____ are dead

- _____ are *DEAD BROKE!!!*

Why are 52% of the people who retire at age 65 broke???
- Lack of proper health insurance
- Lack of proper disability insurance
- Excessive debt
- Lack of saving
- Loss of job
- Lack of proper life insurance on family provider(s)
- Invested too conservatively

**What is the biggest reason why so
many people end up dead broke at retirement?**

They _____! (See answer key below.)

---

*"Procrastination is my sin; it brings me constant
sorrow. I really shouldn't practice it;
perhaps I'll stop tomorrow!"*

Answers: 1, 23, 25, 24, 27
Procrastinated!

The Price of Procrastination

It may seem that procrastination is a low cost option. By ignoring something, it might go away. No action, no cost, right?

That's not how it works with your finances. Your lack of use of your greatest ally, time, can *literally* cost you dearly.

Take a look at the following example. Here's a comparison of the retirement saving behavior of a set of twins.

AGE	Annie	AGE	Abbie
30 ↓ 35	Annie began saving $2,000/year for 6 years when she was 30 years old, for a total of $12,000 of her own money. She earns 10% per year on her money until she's 65 years old.	30 ↓ 40	Abbie didn't save anything during her 30's for retirement, but instead put that money into new furniture, drapes, landscaping and a car.
36 ↓ 65	Annie then doesn't save anything more for retirement from the time she's 36 until she's 65 years old.	41 ↓ 65	At age 40, Abbie begins saving $2,000/year for the next 25 years for a total of $50,000 of her own money. She earns 10% per year on her investments.
	When Annie retires, she has accumulated approximately $245,000.		When Abbie retires, she has accumulated approximately $197,000.

Starting to save for retirement sooner is like buying your retirement on sale. In Annie's case, she not only ended up with more, but she bought her retirement for 75% LESS than what Abbie paid for hers!

Let's look now at how the financial planning process in this workbook can help you overcome procrastination.

The Financial
Planning Process

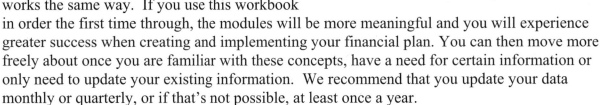

The financial planning process is similar to processes used in games. There are rules you need to follow in order for the game to be understandable and enjoyable for all involved. For example, in baseball you need to run the bases in order - from first to second, second to third and then on to home.

The process for creating a solid financial plan works the same way. If you use this workbook in order the first time through, the modules will be more meaningful and you will experience greater success when creating and implementing your financial plan. You can then move more freely about once you are familiar with these concepts, have a need for certain information or only need to update your existing information. We recommend that you update your data monthly or quarterly, or if that's not possible, at least once a year.

Just a couple of hours a week for 6-8 weeks with the **Controlling Your Financial Future** financial planning process will help you:

In order to get the most from this workbook the first time through, we recommend completing the modules in the order found.

First Base: *Determine Where You Are By:*
  a) Reviewing your insurance coverage (risk management)
  b) Creating a net worth statement

Second Base: *Determine Where You Want To Go By:*
  a) Setting values-based goals

Third Base: *Confidently Accomplish Your Goals By:*
  a) Reducing and eliminating debt
  b) Utilizing powerful and easy to use wealth building techniques

Home: *Implement Your Plan By:*
  a) Creating and implementing a budget that incorporates all of the above
  b) Creating and implementing your personal action plan

At the end of each section of this book, we will stop and direct you to record your Action Ideas on this Action Plan. When you have completed the workbook, tear this page out and post it on your refrigerator, your bathroom mirror, or keep it with your monthly bills as a reminder to complete the actions you have determined during the program.

My Action Plan

First Base

Determine Where You Are

Quick Check Financial Assessment (page 11)

Actions I Need To Take	**Target Date**
1) Check PCUSA policy - emergency funds, & disability coverage	Nov. 30
2) Update PDB to include Elmer & Kids	Nov. 30
3) Videotape house & possessions; burn on DVD	Dec. 20
4) Get info. from Beli re: lawyer for will, living will & durable power of attorney	Dec. 10
5) Create will, living will & durable power of attorney	Jan. 1

Net Worth Actions to Take (page 29)

My Net Worth Isn't As Strong As It Could Be Because:	*Ways to Strengthen My Net Worth:*
We don't have savings	Start college savings
We don't have investments	Start investing, even modestly

With my next raise I will: _____

With my next windfall I will: invest & save _____

7

Determine Where You Want to Go

Values-Based Goal Setting:

In the next one to three years, it is very important to me that I accomplish the following goals (page 41):

	Goal	Total Amount Needed	Amount Needed Per Month
1)	_____	_____	_____
2)	_____	_____	_____
3)	_____	_____	_____

How to Confidently Accomplish Your Goals

Wealth-building techniques that I will use to help me meet my goals (pages 45 to 64):

	Technique	Application	Goal
Example:	Debt Reduction	Consolidate Debt	Eliminate Credit Card Debt
1)	_____	_____	_____
2)	_____	_____	_____
3)	_____	_____	_____

Implement Your Plan

From the spending plan worksheets on pages 75 to 79:

I can find $_____ per month to apply towards my goals.

I will begin using my spending plan as of _____ (month & year).

First Base: Determine Where You Are

The *QUICK CHECK* Financial Assessment

This assessment is designed to spot potential holes in your financial security where you might be vulnerable or lacking an important element of your financial base. Unexpected emergencies that occur can find you unprotected and severely disrupt or undermine your family's security or standard of living now or in retirement.

Part I   identifies possible areas of need based on general, minimum recommended levels of coverage. These are *general guidelines only*; they are not intended nor held out to be recommendations for action.

Part II   provides further clarification and more in-depth reasoning behind the general rule, allowing you to determine if you need to address that area further.

> Every individual's personal financial situation is different, and before you act upon any of these basic guidelines, we recommend you consult a professional with that area of expertise.

The Quick Check
Financial Assessment

Please circle "yes', "no" or "not sure" on each of the following items. When you're through, go to Part II on page 14.

ITEM #	DO YOU HAVE:		COVERED?			
1	**EMERGENCY SAVINGS** of at least three to six months' necessary expenses? These funds should be liquid and easily accessible.		(NO)	YES	NOT SURE	
2	**GROUP (usually employer-provided) SHORT-TERM DISABILITY COVERAGE** for up to six months or one year of disability? You should have coverage that would supply at least 60% of your monthly gross pay.	YOU:	(NO)	YES	NOT SURE	N/A
		SPOUSE:	(NO)	YES	NOT SURE	N/A
3	**GROUP (usually employer-provided) LONG-TERM DISABILITY COVERAGE** for disabilities that last until age 65 or life? You should have coverage that would supply at least 60% of your monthly gross pay. Group disability payments are subject to taxation as ordinary income.	YOU:	NO	YES	(NOT SURE)	N/A
		SPOUSE:	(NO)	YES	NOT SURE	N/A
4	**PERSONAL DISABILITY COVERAGE** if your employer does not provide sufficient disability coverage? Elimination periods vary. These policies provide approximately 50% to 60% of your gross monthly pay. Personal disability insurance is not subject to income tax.	YOU:	(NO)	YES	NOT SURE	N/A
		SPOUSE:	(NO)	YES	NOT SURE	N/A
5	**LIFE INSURANCE COVERAGE** if you have debts or dependents? A <u>general</u> rule of thumb is to have five to seven times the annual value of your services, whether you are employed or are a homemaker.	YOU:	NO	(YES)	NOT SURE	N/A
		SPOUSE:	(NO)	YES	NOT SURE	N/A

ITEM #	DO YOU HAVE:		COVERED?			
6	**HEALTH INSURANCE COVERAGE** that covers at least 80% of out-of-hospital expenses, 80% of doctor's charges and 100% of hospitalization and has an overall payment cap of not less than $1,000,000 (i.e., 80/80/100 coverage?)	YOU:	(YES)	NO	NOT SURE	N/A
		SPOUSE:	(YES)	NO	NOT SURE	N/A
		CHILDREN:	(YES)	NO	NOT SURE	N/A
7	**AUTO INSURANCE** that provides at least $100,000 liability coverage, $300,000 total injury coverage and $50,000 coverage for total property damage (i.e., 100/300/50)?	CAR 1:	YES	NO	NOT SURE	(N/A)
		CAR 2:	YES	NO	NOT SURE	(N/A)
		CAR 3:	YES	NO	NOT SURE	N/A
8	Have you chosen <u>not</u> to buy **CREDIT INSURANCE** policies on any outstanding loans? Credit insurance is offered by banks, car dealerships, and finance companies to cover your loan payment on a car, boat, home, etc. in the event of your disability or death.	YOU:	YES	(NO)	NOT SURE	N/A
		SPOUSE:	YES	(NO)	NOT SURE	N/A
9	**PERSONAL LIABILITY** coverage, also known as an umbrella policy? Standard policy coverage begins at $1 million. If you have an outdoor pool or other potentially dangerous property, teen drivers, a net worth in excess of $100,000 or a high future earnings potential (i.e. a free agent in baseball?), you should have an umbrella policy.	HOME 1:	YES	(NO)	NOT SURE	N/A
		HOME 2:	YES	(NO)	NOT SURE	N/A
10	**HOMEOWNER'S OR TENANT'S INSURANCE?** Both of these are available in fairly standard policies known as HO-1 through HO-6, all of which have different coverages available. Special possessions may require additional riders.	HOME 1:	(YES)	NO	NOT SURE	N/A
		HOME 2:	YES	NO	NOT SURE	(N/A)
11	**PICTURES,** a written household inventory and/or receipts of home improvements and contents stored somewhere outside your home?	HOME 1:	YES	(NO)	NOT SURE	N/A
		HOME 2:	YES	NO	NOT SURE	(N/A)

ITEM #	DO YOU HAVE:		COVERED?			
12	**REPLACEMENT AND INFLATION ENDORSEMENT OPTIONS** on your homeowner's or tenant's insurance? You should have protection that pays you at least 80% of what it takes to replace your loss and an inflation endorsement on your policy.	HOME 1: HOME 2:	YES YES	NO NO	(NOT SURE) NOT SURE	N/A (N/A)
13	**UPDATED BENEFICIARIES** of bank, brokerage and retirement accounts and reviewed titles to property ownership within the last three years to reflect any deaths, divorces, marriages or children?	YOU: SPOUSE:	YES YES	NO NO	(NOT SURE) NOT SURE	N/A (N/A)
14	A **WILL?** Wills should be updated every three years and revised for changes such as marriage, divorces, births, death, relocation and changes in business situations or tax laws.	YOU: SPOUSE:	YES YES	(NO) (NO)	NOT SURE NOT SURE	N/A N/A
15	A **DURABLE POWER OF ATTORNEY?** This lets someone act for you even if you're judged senile or mentally disabled.	YOU: SPOUSE:	YES YES	(NO) (NO)	NOT SURE NOT SURE	N/A N/A
16	A **LIVING WILL/PATIENT ADVOCATE?** A living will allows you to appoint someone to exercise your right to refuse treatment that artificially prolongs your dying.	YOU: SPOUSE:	YES YES	(NO) (NO)	NOT SURE NOT SURE	N/A N/A
17	A need for **ESTATE PLANNING?** In 2005, if your assets exceed $1.5 million for an individual or $3.0 million for a married couple, your estate will be subject to substantial estate taxes. The estate exclusion amount per person increases to $2.0 million per individual for 2006-2008.	YOU: SPOUSE:	YES YES	NO NO	NOT SURE NOT SURE	(N/A) (N/A)

Review of "NO" Responses to the Quick Check Financial Assessment

Check off the left-hand boxes for all items you answered "no" or "not sure" to in Part I. Then read through the items you checked off to see if you need to take further action. If so, record that item on your Action Plan and commit to taking action within 30 days!

CHECK IF ANSWERED "NO" OR "NOT SURE"	TOPIC	CHECK IF ACTION IS NEEDED

1. **EMERGENCY SAVINGS:**

These funds should be liquid and easily accessible. A reserve fund is essentially self-insurance. Minor costs and claims can be expensive to insure; the more savings you have, the less insurance you need. For example, you can increase your car deductibles, eliminate children's life insurance or reduce or eliminate short-term disability policies when you have adequate savings. Three to six months of <u>necessary expenses</u> are highly recommended.

check PCUSA policy for mission co-workers

2. **GROUP SHORT-TERM DISABILITY:**

Ninety percent of all disabilities are short-term and last about 13 weeks. If you have an adequate emergency fund or your household does not depend on your income or services, then you do not need this policy. If it is available to you through your employer then take advantage of it, since a short-term disability could use up all of your savings. If you need to consider a short-term disability policy but a group plan isn't available to you, review the personal disability policy in item #4.

YOU: _____
SPOUSE: _____

3. **GROUP LONG-TERM DISABILITY:**

Your chances of becoming permanently disabled are <u>five times greater than dying prematurely.</u> A person disabled permanently is a greater financial strain on a family than a person who dies. Again, if your family depends on your income or services and you don't have emergency savings set aside or a personal disability policy, you should ask your benefits department to sign you up. If you don't have group disability available to you, and/or if your family depends on your spouse's income or services and they are not covered by a group plan, review item #4.

review PCUSA policy

YOU: _____
SPOUSE: _____

4. ☑ **PERSONAL DISABILITY COVERAGE:**

If you contribute to the household and you are not covered by a group plan, purchase a personal disability policy. Rarely does a family have the financial resources to handle the economic strain of a long-term disability. The elimination period you choose will depend greatly on the amount of savings you have built up. The longer the elimination period the lower your policy costs will be. Get coverage that is equivalent to 60-65% of your current annual income; make sure the policy is noncancellable and covers you for your "own occupation", meaning that if you become disabled, the insurance company will pay if you can't return to what you were doing before. If you don't get "own occupation" coverage, the insurance company will stop paying if you are mobile enough to empty waste baskets and do light cleaning. Also be sure your coverage is to age 65 or for life.

YOU: _____
SPOUSE: _____

5. ☐ **LIFE INSURANCE:**

If you have debts and/or dependents, buy life insurance. There are two main types of life insurance: term or cash value. Cash value policies such as whole life, universal life, and variable life vary in the way the savings portion feature of the policy is invested and whether you or the insurance company accepts the risk of the value of the investment. Term policies provide "pure" life insurance for people who cannot afford or do not desire the savings feature involved in "cash value" policies. The amount and type you require will depend on your income level, number of dependents, special family needs, outstanding debts and financial goals such as sending all of your children to college, etc. Most Americans are severely under-insured. If you are employed outside of the home, most employers do provide some amount of life insurance automatically; $50,000 is a common amount. This should not be your primary insurance if you have dependents. It can be factored into your personal life insurance needs, however, and help reduce the coverage that you need. If you are single with no dependents and little debt, group life can be sufficient until your lifestyle becomes more complicated. If you are a non-working spouse, you still need enough coverage to pay for the services you provide to your family in the event of your death.

ODB for Elmer & kids

YOU: _____
SPOUSE: _____

6. ☐ **HEALTH INSURANCE:**

If you or any member of your family does not have health insurance, GET IT!!! First, if any member of the family is on an employer-provided plan, see if you can add other family members to it. Next, contact trade or professional organizations you belong to or could join. These often have group health coverage available to members. Lastly, pursue a personal policy. Some health insurers have open enrollment periods where you do not have to pass a health exam to join.

YOU: _____
SPOUSE _____
CHILD: _____

7. ☐ **AUTO INSURANCE:**

An important aspect of auto insurance is liability coverage to protect your wealth in the event that the driver of your car proved to be negligent in an accident. You can be sued for injury, property damage, loss of income and pain and suffering. Liability coverage covers these possibilities as well as legal costs. Consider higher uninsured and underinsured coverage to protect you from those who do not have any insurance at all - the investment is minimal for much greater protection.

8. ☑ **CREDIT INSURANCE:**

Credit insurance is very overpriced. It's an additional source of income for the issuer with low cost, like selling you a service warranty on a new refrigerator. Instead of having specific insurance coverage on your loans, you should factor your debts into your need for life insurance.

9. ☑ **PERSONAL LIABILITY COVERAGE:**

Umbrella policies for $1,000,000 cost on average around $200 per year. If your assets are under $100,000 and you don't have any unusual risk exposure, then the standard liability on your home should be sufficient coverage. If your net worth exceeds $100,000 or if you have high risk exposure, an umbrella policy can provide important additional coverage.

10. ☐ **HOMEOWNER'S OR TENANT'S INSURANCE:**

Most homeowners are required to have insurance and it is incorporated into the mortgage payment. Tenants or apartment dwellers are not required to be insured; only one out of every five renters insures his personal property. Coverage includes not only fire but theft and other perils caused by weather. Tenants policies only cost about $10-$15 per month.

11. ☑ **PROOF OF YOUR HOUSEHOLD POSSESSIONS:**

Recent natural disasters are always a poignant reminder of the importance of having a home inventory. At a minimum, videotape your entire home; open drawers, closets, cabinets, etc. Take pictures from a close enough range to show all the contents. Make overall views of your rooms and what's in them. Remember to get the garage, attic, landscaping, tool shed, etc. Talk about each item as you show it, recording the model and price on tape. Your inventory is your guarantee that you'll collect all the protection you paid for. With it, you can make a full list of all your losses. Insurers will generally accept a list you reconstruct from memory. But you'll never recall every item, and those little things add up. When buying insurance most people focus only on their few expensive pieces of furniture. But what drives up the price of refurnishing a home is the pencils and potholders, jackets and mittens, baseballs and houseplants, and other common household items.

videotape home, possessions w/ costs, etc.

12.☑ HOMEOWNER'S INFLATION ENDORSEMENT:

Newer policies usually have an inflation endorsement policy but older policies might not. Homes should be insured based on replacement value, the standard policy being 80% of fair market value. A portion of your home value is the land which is indestructible, and the foundation which is nearly indestructible. Since replacement costs go up every year, instead of upping your policy each year, an inflation endorsement automatically increases your coverage with the rise in construction costs and building code changes.

find out from Metropolitana

_____

13.☑ BENEFICIARIES AND PROPERTY OWNERSHIP:

Designated beneficiaries are almost an invisible clause on any bank or brokerage account. Once the original paperwork is done and filed away, you are rarely reminded of who you had listed on your accounts. Death, divorce, marriage and additional children will normally cause beneficiaries to be changed, but this process is often overlooked and the intended party suffers. Also, property owned jointly skips probate (a time-consuming legal process), while individually-owned property in an estate must go through probate.

review ODB (write BOP?)

YOU: _____
SPOUSE: _____

14.☑ WILLS:

If you die without a will, your estate will be divided up by the state according to the state laws of intestacy. If you are single, this usually means the state will distribute your assets first to your surviving parents, then equally to your siblings. If you are married, this means (in most states) that your spouse will receive one third to one half of your estate and any children would equally split the rest. It also means the state would choose guardians for your children if both of you should unexpectedly die. Lastly, the state chooses an administrator for your estate settlement when no will exists. Wills allow your wishes to be executed and your surviving dependents/family/friends to be cared for in the way you see fit. It is also recommended that you draft a "letter of instruction" that details where important documents are located and what you would like done about your burial.

ask Beli re: who did their will.

YOU: _____
SPOUSE: _____

15.☑ DURABLE POWER OF ATTORNEY:

Everyone needs a backup - a person to act for you if you're away, if you're sick, if you get hit by a car and can't function for a while, or if you grow senile. That means giving someone - a spouse, a parent, an adult child, a trusted friend - your power of attorney. A durable power of attorney lasts, while other powers don't. As long as you are mentally capable, you can revoke a durable power whenever you like. You have to execute a new durable power every four or five years, to show that your intention holds. Insurance companies and financial institutions probably won't honor an old power.
If you'd rather not trust anyone until you absolutely have to, write a springing power of attorney. It doesn't take effect unless you become mentally incapacitated, and the document defines exactly what that means.

YOU: _____
SPOUSE: _____

First Base: Determine Where You Are

16. ☑ **LIVING WILL/PATIENT ADVOCATE:**

look online

Anyone who has seen a dying or comatose parent hooked up to life-support machines understands the issue of the right to die. Decision making for the family is difficult under times of great emotional stress. The situation can become one that also impacts family finances. The medical action that is or is not taken under those circumstances can be one dictated by the patient, <u>provided</u> the situation has been fully considered while of sound mind and body. Please make clear your views to your immediate family and physicians. Most states have available "Living Wills" and/or durable powers of attorney for health care. Contact your local bar association for more information.

YOU: _____
SPOUSE: _____

17. ☑ **ESTATE PLANNING:**

N/A

For 2005, for an individual with assets exceeding $1.5 million after debts have been satisfied, or a married couple with assets exceeding $3.0 million after their debts have been satisfied, an estate planner can help you employ the tax savings strategies most suitable for your situation. Strategies include giving your assets away while you are alive to intended beneficiaries, creating trusts to generate income for your needs and gifting assets to charitable institutions. Gifting and utilizing trusts require careful and professional planning. The level of assets excluded from federal estate taxation increases in 2006-2008 to reach a level of $2.0 million per person and eventually $3.5 million per person in 2009.

YOU: _____
SPOUSE: _____

<u>*Stop Here*</u>
Record your answers on your Action Plan on page 7 before moving on.

Your Net Worth Assessment

The second part of determining where you are is to assess your existing financial condition, i.e., what have you accumulated thus far in terms of assets and debts?

In sum, your net worth is a snapshot of all the financial decisions you have made through today. This means that every time you buy unplanned extras at the grocery store or indulge in that great tool sale at Sears, you decrease the amount of money available to pay on debt or increase your savings, which in turn affects what your net worth could be now and in the future.

In particular, we will cover in this section:

Part I: What is net worth? How did I get it? What should I do with it?

Part II: Enter the values of what you own and what you owe, and find out your net worth!

Part III: Net Worth Analysis

- Analyze what you own, owe, and what's left over.

- Get ideas for how to improve your net worth.

- Update your Action Plan.

Part IV: Compare your net worth to the national averages.

Part I: What Is Net Worth?
How Did I Get It?
What Should I Do With It?

Let's say your company transferred you to Europe to work for the next ten years. So you decide it will be easier to sell off everything you own, pay off all your debts and just buy what you need once there.

The money you would have left over is your net worth!

More formally, your net worth is the value of what <u>you</u> own today (meaning what other people would pay, not what you think it is worth!) less the value of what you owe (mortgages, car loans, credit cards, student loans, etc.).

Your Net Worth = the Value of What You Own
Less the Value of What You Owe.

If you think about it, *every* financial decision you make affects your net worth. Thomas Stanley and William Danko, authors of "The Millionaire Next Door", suggest as a rule of thumb your net worth should be your age times your annual income divided by 10. If your net worth is more than that, then you are doing better than your peers at managing your money. If your net worth is less than that, you need to learn more about managing your finances now to begin maximizing what you will have in the future.

You should use your net worth as a report card to see how well you are progressing financially. Calculate your net worth at least once a year. If your net worth hasn't increased at least 10% over the prior year, then you need to seriously reconsider how you are spending your money. What counts is what we keep, not what we earn!

How the Choices You Make Affect Your Wealth

Spending That *Helps* Your Net Worth

Owning a home

Saving

Spending That *Hurts* Your Net Worth

Spending using credit cards

Buying new cars

Spending That Neither Hurts Nor Helps Your Net Worth

Food; eating out

Buying new clothing

Test: Circle which answer you think is correct. *(The answers are at the bottom of the page.)*

- If you spend money on a car, and the value of that car decreases over time, it will (hurt or help) your net worth.
- If you buy a home, your net worth will (decrease or increase) over time since home values increase.
- If you buy $500 of clothing on credit, and don't pay it off immediately, you (increase or decrease) your net worth, since you now owe more money.
- If you paid $100 for basketball tickets, it has (no or much) effect on your net worth at all since they have no lasting value (memories excluded).

Key: hurt, increase, decrease, no

21

Part II: Calculating Your Net Worth

Remember:

> Your Net Worth = the Value of What You Own
> Less the Value of What You Owe.

To make it easier for you to complete this section, take a few minutes right now to gather all recent statements for your 401(k), IRAs, checking and savings accounts, mutual funds, brokerage accounts, mortgage balance, credit card balances, etc.

We'll start by collecting information on the items you own. These items are broken into five categories:

- liquid
- loaned
- owned
- personal
- deferred assets.

This makes it easier to record and later analyze your information. By the way, you're not expected to have a value for every category. Since financial situations vary, we have to include all possibilities.

The following pages will explain each category and guide you through collecting your numbers.

Calculating Your Net Worth: Liquid Assets

Liquid Assets are investments where your money can be converted into cash in hand very easily. Check your most recent statements and fill in current values for those areas where you have that type of investment.

Liquid Assets		
Comments	I/WE OWN	Name of Item
Amount on Hand	$	Cash
	$	Checking Accounts
	$	Savings Accounts
	$	Money Market Funds
Cash Value	$	Whole-Life Life Insurance
Total	$	**Transfer this total to LINE A on page 29**

Calculating Your Net Worth: Loaned Assets

Loaned Assets are investments where you have "loaned" your money to a financial institution or person with the expectation you will receive all your money back (after a certain amount of time), plus interest.

Check your most recent statements and fill in the current values for those areas below where you have that type of investment.

Comments	I/WE OWN	Name of Item
		Loaned Assets
Comments	I/WE OWN	Name of Item
Face Value	$	Certificates of Deposit
Face Value	$	U.S. Treasury Bills, Notes or Bonds
	$	U.S. Government Bond Mutual Funds
	$	U.S. Savings Bonds
	$	Corporate Bonds
	$	Corporate Bond Mutual Funds
	$	Municipal Bonds
	$	Municipal Bond Mutual Funds
	$	Notes Receivable
	$	Collectible Debts
	$	Other
Balance Due You	$	Land Contracts
Total	$ 0	**Transfer this total to LINE B on page 29**

Calculating Your Net Worth: Owned Assets

Owned Assets are investments where you have actual "ownership." These types of investments are expected to increase in value over time, allowing you to benefit from their higher values.

Check your most recent statements and fill in the current values in those areas below where you have that type of investment.

NOTE: The estimated value of an asset should be the amount you will get if you sell it today to a "reasonable" buyer.

Owned Assets		
Comments	I/WE OWN	Name of Item
Market Value	$	Common and preferred stocks
	$	Stock mutual funds
	$ 60,000	Your primary home
	$	Your second/vacation home
	$	Investment property (like rentals), limited partnerships
	$	Business interest(s)
	$	Gold & silver (other than jewelry)
	$	Collectibles (art, collections, etc.)
	$	Jewelry (investment quality)
Total	$ 60,000	**Transfer this total to LINE C on page 29**

Calculating Your Net Worth: Personal Assets

Personal Assets are those that decrease in value over time due to wear and tear, obsolescence, depreciation, etc.

NOTE: The estimated value of an asset should be the amount you will get if you sell it today.

Personal Assets		
Comments	I/WE OWN	Name of Item
Estimated Fair Market Value	$12,000	Automobiles
	$	Boats, motorcycles, ski doos, etc.
	$ 800	Home furnishings
	$ 500	Computer & peripherals, other electronics
	$	Jewelry (not investment quality)
	$	Equipment, tools, lawnmowers, etc.
Total	$ 13,300	**Transfer this total to LINE D on page 29**

Calculating Your Net Worth: Deferred Assets

Deferred Assets are those investments or amounts you have set aside for a future purpose like retirement, college, etc.

Check your most recent statements and fill in the areas below where you have that type of investment.

Deferred Assets		
Comments	I/WE OWN	Name of Item
Vested or Cash Value	$	IRA's
	$	Keogh and/or SEP accounts
	$	Profit sharing plans/401(k)/403(b)/457 plans
	$	Vested pension plans
	$	Deferred compensation
	$	Annuities
Est. Value	$	College funding
Est. Value	$	Trusts and inheritances
Total	$ 0	**Transfer the total to LINE E on page 29**

Calculating Your Net Worth: Liabilities or Money That Is Owed

Liabilities are monies you owe someone else. For many people, it is a sign of past consumption that they are still paying for now. The more debt you have, the less peace of mind and contentment you experience with money overall.

Amounts You Owe		
Name of Item	I/We Owe	Interest Rate Charged
Credit card: _____	$ 5,300	0 %
Credit card: _____	$	%
Credit card: _____	$	%
Credit card: _____	$	%
Total Short-Term Debt (less than 1 year) **Transfer this total to LINE F on page 29**	$ 5,300	
Vehicle Loan 1	$ 5,700	10 %
Vehicle Loan 2	$ 600	0 %
Bank Installment Loans	$	%
Student Loans	$	%
Total Intermediate-Term Debt (1-5 years) **Transfer this total to LINE G on page 29**	$	
First Mortgage	$	%
Second Mortgage	$	%
Long-Term Debt (over 5 years) **Transfer this total to LINE H on page 29**	$ 16,000	6 %
Total Owed	$ 27,600	

Net Worth Summary

Finish transferring the values of each section listed below from the prior worksheets. See the example in the appendix for more information.

	Estimated Current Value	As a % of Total Assets	Estimated Average Return Earned
I) What You Own (Assets):			
A) Total Liquid Assets . . . .(from page 23)	$ _____	_____ %	1-4%
B) Total Loaned Assets . . . . (from page 24)	_____	_____	3-7%
C) Total Owned Assets . . . .(from page 25)	60,000	_____	6-12%
D) Total Personal Assets . . . . (from page 26)	13,300	_____	-20% or more per year
E) Total Deferred & Special Assets .(from page 27)	_____	_____	6-12%
Total Assets, or What You Own	$ 73,300	100 %	

	Estimated Balance	As a % of Total Debts	Average Interest Rate Paid
II) What You Owe (Liabilities):			
F) Total Short-Term Debt . . . .(from page 28)	$ 5,300	_____ %	12-23%
G) Total Intermediate-Term Debt . .(from page 28)	6,300	_____	6-12%
H) Total Long-Term Debt . . . .(from page 28)	16,000	_____	5-9%
Total Liabilities, or What You Owe	$ 27,600	100 %	

YOUR NET WORTH = $ 45,700

OWN (I) – OWE (II)

Part III: Is Your Net Worth As Strong As It Could Be?

Take a moment to analyze the condition of your current financial situation. Looking at your net worth statement on the prior page:

1) Do you have <u>less</u> than three to six months' necessary expenses in liquid assets? (Take a guess.) If yes, you're risking not having enough cash if an emergency arises.

    Y

    Y   or   N

2) Do you have more than 25% of your total assets in one single asset or investment (other than your home)? If so, you have too many eggs in one basket and should better diversify (spread out) your money among other investments.

    N/A

    Y   or   N

3) Is the interest rate you're paying on credit cards more than what you are earning on your savings? If yes, your borrowing costs are greater than the interest you're earning and you're wasting money, so use some of your savings to pay off your debts as quickly as possible.

    Y   or   N

4) Is your credit card debt plus your debt on cars or furniture more than a 1/3 of your net worth? If so, you may be insolvent. If you don't expect higher earnings over the next 3-5 years to help correct this, begin a debt reduction plan and/or seek credit counseling immediately.

    N

    Y   or   N

Stop Here

Record your answers on your Action Plan on page 7 before moving on.

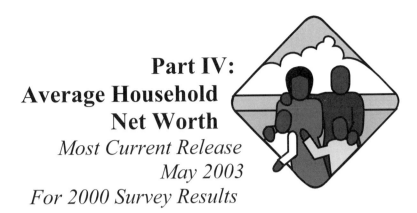

Part IV:
Average Household
Net Worth
Most Current Release
May 2003
For 2000 Survey Results

Here's more information to help you gauge how far you've already come in your financial management.

	Less Than 35	35 - 44	45 - 54	55 - 64	65 or Older
Average Net Worth . . .	$7,240	$44,275	$83,150	$112,048	$108,885
		45,700			
Average Value of Assets Held:					
Interest-Earning Deposits	1,500	2,760	4,000	7,000	10,000
Other Interest-Earning Assets	--	23,210	20,000	23,210	30,000
Regular Checking Accounts	500	600	700	700	700
Stock and Mutual Funds	6,000	14,000	20,000	36,000	40,000
Equity in Business/Profession	7,000	6,700	10,000	10,000	20,000
Equity in Home	22,000	40,500	60,000	78,000	85,000
401k and Thrift Savings Plan	7,500	21,200	31,290	38,000	33,000

Source: U.S. Department of Commerce, Bureau of the Census

Asset Ownership of Households: 2000
Revised: 2005

First Base: Determine Where You Are

Second Base: Determine Where You Want to Go

Values-Based Goal Setting

Here's where you begin taking control of your financial future. In this section we will cover:

Part I: The importance of having meaningful goals.

Part II: What's important to you?

Part III: Identify and prioritize your list of possible goals based on your values.

Part IV: Determine your specific spending priorities for the next twelve months.

- Prioritize your six top goals and print reports.

- Explore ideas for finding dollars to redirect toward your goals.

- Update your Action Plan.

What is Values-Based Goal Setting?
Why are Goals Important?

Remember what we said earlier? The number one reason why people reach age 65 "dead broke" (meaning they depend on friends and family or have to work to survive) is procrastination.

Procrastination affects us in all areas of life, not just with money. It creeps in when we should be studying, when we should be dieting, when we need to exercise, and when it's time to clean the house.

The best way to overcome procrastination is to identify meaningful goals that are based on key personal values. This will help pull you through when the going gets rough. Meaningful goals allow us to say "no" in order to help us stay on track. Imagine being responsible for steering a boat when you didn't know where you were supposed to go. Silly, isn't it? Yet we do this all the time with our financial future.

The following exercises are to help you overcome procrastination and to increase the amount of peace of mind and contentment you experience with your money. It's also a great tool for spouses, newlyweds or anyone that has to share financial decision-making with a significant other. Have both parties complete the exercises and then jointly finish the "Spending Priorities" plan. It's a great way to open the lines of financial communication. You're bound to find out things you didn't know!

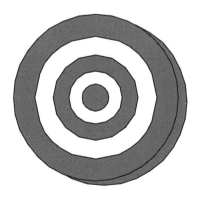

What's Important to You?

The first place to start when creating meaningful goals is to define what success means to you. Is it fame, fortune, or recognition? Or is it your relationship with God, your children, or your spouse?

The following chart depicts the results of a survey conducted by the Roper Organization in the early 1990's. It represents the percent of men and women who believe selected achievements express the idea of success. For these respondents, being a good spouse and parent was the most common measure of success. Women were more likely than men to define success in religious terms.

Take a minute to identify which three of the following items define success for you. Circle and number your top three choices (1, 2, and 3). Then transfer these items to page 39.

A Measure of Success

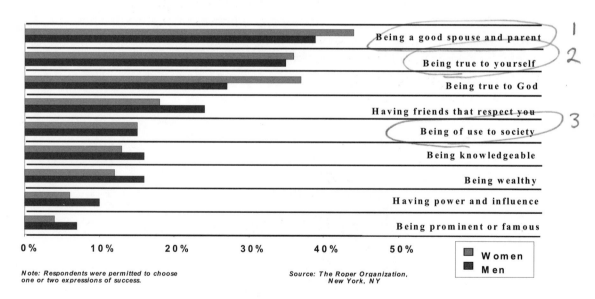

Note: Respondents were permitted to choose one or two expressions of success.

Source: The Roper Organization, New York, NY

Source: American Demographics, March 1991
Reprinted with permission

Identifying Possible Goals

We will now lead you through a process that will help you identify your goals.

Keeping in mind the top three items from the prior page that define success for you, complete the worksheet on the next page by:

1. Circling anything that is a goal for you in the left hand column.

2. Placing a check mark in one of the three white columns: is it an essential goal, important goal, or just a nice goal?

3. Choosing three to five goals within each category. For example, you can choose up to five goals in the essential column, five goals in the important column and five goals in the nice column. Number them "1" for most important, "2" for next most important, etc.

Second Base: Determine Where You Want to Go

List of Potential Goals

1) Circle all those goals that are important to you
2) Place a checkmark for each goal as to whether it is essential, important, or nice
3) Rate the goals within each category (essential, important, nice) by numbering them 1–5, with 1 being most important.

Goal	Essential		Important		Nice	
New house or bigger house						
Second house (vacation home, time share unit, etc.)						
Interior home improvement (furniture, appliances, redecorating)			✓	1.		
Exterior home improvement (landscaping, roofing, additions, etc.)	✓	1				
New car or second car			✓	3		
Recreational vehicles (mobile homes, boat, snowmobiles, etc.)						
Home electronics (stereo, VCR, computer, etc.)						
New clothing						
Enrichment programs for children (ballet, music, sports, etc.)			✓	2		
Vacation or major travel/adventure programs			✓	5		
Gifts for grandchildren, spouse, family, etc.						
Emergency savings						
Debt reduction	✓	3.				
Personal (taxable) investment program						
401(k) or other retirement fund	✓	5				
College fund for children			✓	4		
Continuing education (college enrichment)						
Will and estate plan drawn up	✓	4				
Start/expand a business						
Career change (anticipated income reduction or expansion)						
Quality of life (sacrificing additional income to be with family)	✓	2				
New hobby (crafts, sports, building things, etc.)						
Increase charitable contributions						
Volunteering more time to church, non-profit organizations, etc.						
Other						
Other						

Identifying
Needs vs. Wants

Most of us don't have the money or the time to tackle all of our potential goals at the same time. The point of this exercise is to bring more focus to the list you created on the prior page by identifying which goals are needs and which are wants.

The way to successfully accomplish your goals is to match your potential goals to the values you identified earlier. This way, the goals are more meaningful and you will be more motivated to make them happen.

Record your top three values from page 36 in the left hand column. Then try to match your essential and important goals to one or more of your top personal values. Finish by evaluating your list and assigning a goal number of 1-6. Those that didn't make the top six for now will have to wait until you've completed one or more of the items on this list first.

Top Personal Values	*Description of Goal*	*Goal Number*
1) Being a good spouse & parent	• Quality of life *no dollar value*	1
	• Vacation (family visits)	6
@ of life & enrichment prog. u $400	• Enrichment programs for children	3
@ of life & enrichment prog. ap together	• College fund for children	
2) Being true to self	• Interior home improvement	4
	• Debt reduction	5
minimal? cost?	(• Wills estate planning	2)
	• 401 k	
3) Being of use to society	• _____	___
	• _____	___
	• _____	___
	• _____	___

Second Base: Determine Where You Want to Go

Your Spending Priorities

Now you need to further refine which goals you will start with first. Most people only have the budget and the emotions to effectively handle up to six goals at any one time. You may even want to just start with one or two – especially if they involve large dollar amounts. Once that goal is reached it will free up a sizable monthly sum that can be redirected to accomplishing several of your other goals.

1. On the bottom line, enter the most important goal you identified on the prior page (Column 1).

2. Then fill in the dollars you will need to reach that goal (Column 2).

3. In addition, fill in the number of months in which you want that goal accomplished (Column 3).

4. Divide the figure in Column 2 by the number of months in Column 3 to arrive at the amount you need per month to put toward that goal.

5. Then fill in the amount you're already putting toward that goal, if any (Column 5).

6. In Column 6 you need to calculate the additional amount needed per month to accomplish that goal. This is done by subtracting the amount in Column 5 from the amount in Column 4. If "the additional amount needed per month" is more than you can handle at this time, go back to step 3 (Column 3) and enter a higher number of months in which to achieve the goal. Repeat as necessary.

7. Total Columns 4, 5, and 6. If those numbers will be a challenge to achieve, go back to Step 3 and enter a higher number of months.

8. You may only be able to afford attacking Goal #1 first. If so, once that goal is accomplished those dollars can then be applied to goals 2, 3, 4, etc.

In order for goals to be accomplished, they need to be SMART:

S pecific

M easurable

A ttainable

R ealistic

T arget date to accomplish

do with Elmer

The following worksheet will help you be SMART with your money. To complete, follow the instructions on the prior page.

(1) Priority Goals	(2) Total Amount Needed	(3) Time Frame (number of months)	(4) Amt. Needed/ Month (Column 2 / Column 3)	(5) Amount Already Allocated	(6) Amount Needed Per Month (Column 4 - Column 5)
Goal #6:					
Goal #5:					
Goal #4:					
Goal #3:					
Goal #2:					
Goal #1:					
Example: Goal #1: Pay off credit cards	$5,000	12	$420	$250	$170/mo.
Totals	$	$		$	$

So Where Do You Find the Money
to Help You Accomplish Your Goals?

Circle those items you could use to help you reach your goals.

- The best thing you can do is to begin using a budget.

- The second best place to uncover dollars for more important goals is to stop *using credit cards*. Pay off what you have outstanding now. Charge no more. In a few months you'll automatically have several hundred dollars more a month. It's like getting a raise!

- Postpone getting that new car for one more year, especially if your car is in relatively good working condition. In addition, don't buy new, buy used! A one year old car with less than 20,000 miles is like buying a new car for 30% off, and with a lower payment.

- Brown bag your lunch three days a week. Six dollars a day times three days a week times four weeks a month is $72 a month, or $864 a year. If you brown bag it five days a week, you can save $1,440 to apply towards more meaningful, long-lasting goals.

- Go back to school and improve your skills to earn more money.

- Shop at garage sales or skim the want ads for children's clothes, tools, appliances, etc.

- Cut back on or cut out fixed and variable expenses. Visit the budgeting (spending plan) section to learn more. If you've never used a budget before, you'll be surprised you can uncover 5-15% of your monthly income going to things that have little meaning to you. Use your goals as your motivation to say "no" and take charge of your financial future.

Stop Here
Record your answers on
your Action Plan on page 7
before moving on.

Third Base:
How to Confidently
Accomplish Your Goals

Third Base: How to Confidently Accomplish Your Goals

How to Build Wealth and Confidently Accomplish Your Goals

Once you've laid your financial foundation (with proper insurance coverage and an estate plan), determined where you are now (net worth), and where you want to go (values-based goals), you can begin to work on accomplishing your goals.

The items included in this section were chosen because if you practice them regularly, you virtually assure the security of your financial future. These particular financial actions give you the greatest benefit in terms of time involved, financial payoff, etc.

These items are:

- Maximizing your contribution to deferred savings plans (401(k)s, 403(b)s, 457 plans)

- Reducing and eliminating consumer debt (anything other than your mortgage)

- Utilizing three, easy-to-use, basic investing principles to get you to your goals sooner, better, with less risk.

Wealth Building:
Taxes and Your Retirement Savings
401(k), 403(b) or 457 plans

If you have a deferred savings retirement plan at work, **TAKE FULL ADVANTAGE OF IT!** In other words, if you're not currently putting in the maximum amount you are allowed, *find a way to do it!* This is <u>BY FAR</u> the easiest, most effective, most profitable way to build wealth for retirement. Your employer has set up the vehicle for you; it comes directly out of your check; they have pre-screened a menu of investments; and they provide you with statements of your progress. How much easier can it get? All that's needed is for you to commit to using it, bite the bullet on current spending, and help it grow! The rate of return to you for participating in one of these plans literally cannot consistently be exceeded by any other investment.

Here's an example of the financial benefit to you of participating in one of these plans:

			Sample	**You**

1) Your dollar contribution:

    <u>15%</u>   X $ <u>45,000</u>   = $ 6,750 $ _____
    (percent contribution)   (annual salary)

2) Your employer's contribution to your plan: (if there is a match)

    $ <u>45,000</u>   X   <u>6%</u>   X   <u>0.50</u>   = $ 1,350 $ _____
    (annual   (employer   (matching
    salary)   contribution rate)   per dollar)

3) Total retirement contribution to your account   = $ 8,100 $ _____
for the year (line 1 + line 2):

4) Tax savings from your tax-deductible contribution:

    <u>.28</u>   X $ <u>6,750</u>   = $ 1,890 $ _____
    (your marginal   (your contribution
    tax rate - see chart)   from line 1)

5) Dollars after taxes you actually contributed: (Line 1-Line 4) = $ 4,860 $ _____

6) Your out of pocket monthly retirement savings   = $ 405/mo. $ _____
(Line 5 divided by 12 months)

7) Your immediate rate of return:

    ($ <u>1,350</u>   plus $ <u>1,890</u>) divided by $ <u>6,750</u>
    employer contrib.   tax savings   dollars you =   48%   %
    (line 2)   (line 4)   initially contributed   **RATE OF RETURN**
               (line 1)

2005 Tax Rate	Married, Separate	Married, Joint	Single	Head of Household
10%	up to $7,300	up to $14,600	up to $7,300	up to $10,450
15%	$7,300 - $29,700	$14,600 - $59,400	$7,300 - $29,700	$10,450 - $39,800
25%	$29,700 - $59,975	$59,400 - $119,950	$29,700 - $71,950	$39,800 - $102,800
28%	$59,975 - $91,400	$119,950 - $182,800	$71,950 - $150,150	$102,800 - $166,450
33%	$91,400 - $163,225	$182,800 - $326,450	$150,150 - $326,450	$166,450 - $326,450
35%	$163,225+	$326,450+	$326,450+	$326,450+

Reduce and Eliminate Debt

In this section, we will take you through the following proven system for reducing and eliminating debt quickly.

Step I: Secrets to Getting Out of Debt.

Step II: List the Debts You Owe.

Step III: Evaluate Your Debt.

Step IV: Create and Work a Plan to Eliminate Debt.

Step I: The Secret to Getting Out of Debt

Occasional debt on a credit card never hurt anyone, but permanent indebtedness to support a spending habit is a terrible waste of energy, time and dollars. It's a loser's game at 18% interest. You overpay for everything when you buy on credit – nearly one-fifth more. Why would you want to throw that much money away? You're living rich while growing poor.

Many people don't try to change their spending behavior unless they are truly motivated to do so. Napoleon Hill, a famous philosopher during the 1960's and 1970's, and author of the book *Think and Grow Rich,* called this the point of "creative dissatisfaction." Sometimes it's not until we get so dissatisfied with something, or are forced to do something because of the alternative circumstances, that we finally create and follow through on a plan. People who suffer a health setback that could be improved by weight loss and healthier eating obviously have a lot of motivation to follow through. For some of us with debt, it may not be until we are in real trouble that we finally get on the ball and do something about it.

In sum: getting and staying out of debt is not easy, since it means changing ingrained behaviors that have been around for a long time. You've got to get back in shape, and it means creating a workout plan and monitoring it closely to do so.

Here are the secrets to getting and staying out of debt:

1. **KNOW WHAT YOU WANT:** Unless you think about, choose, say and do what you really want, you risk getting stuck with a life or financial circumstances you do not desire. Not knowing what you really want keeps you from getting unstuck from a debt-accumulating spending habit.

    Identify something that emotionally and/or intellectually motivates you, and every other member of your household, to say "no" to debt when you need to. It may be the promise of a future reward for yourself on the day you become debt free. Or it may be the hope and belief of repairing and rebuilding your relationships with your spouse and children if debt has created an environment of tension, disagreement, and frustration.

2. **KNOW WHAT YOU HAVE:** Complete the worksheet in Part II so you can know the size and strength of what you're wrestling.

3. **HAVE A PLAN:** Whatever you're paying now on debt, plan to keep on paying it until you're debt free. For instance, once you complete the following worksheet and find you are spending $500 per month on debt repayment, keep on paying $500 per month even though other debts have been paid off.

4. **WORK AND RE-WORK YOUR PLAN:**

Your Warm-Up Exercise: Do not use a credit card for 21 days. Pay only by check or cash. Why 21 days? Studies show that it takes that long to change a behavior. Anything you can do to begin diminishing your reliance on and willingness to use debt will make it that much easier to get and stay out of debt in the future.

Step 2: Update your worksheet with your new balances and planned payment schedule every month. Watching your debt be paid off can actually be emotionally exciting, uplifting and create a sense of hope and control, especially once the little balances get paid off and those dollars can all be re-channeled to paying down other debt.

Now it is time for you to create your plan to become and stay debt free. Take some time right now to gather all your monthly statements (if available) for the following items, and organize them in order of highest interest rate paid to lowest interest rate paid.

- *Credit card statements*
- *Student loan statements*
- *Car loan statements*
- *Mortgage*

You will be recording the current balance (if you haven't already entered the information in the Net Worth section), monthly payment, number of months (term) of the loan, and interest rate information on the worksheet in Part II.

Step II: Reducing Debt
What Do You Owe?

The first step in reducing debt is to determine, in sum, what debts you owe as of today. List them in order of highest interest rate first, along with what you are currently paying per month on each (not the minimum required).

Name of Item	Current Balance	Monthly Payments	Interest Rate Paying
Credit card: _____	$	$	%
Credit card: _____	$	$	%
Credit card: _____	$	$	%
Credit card: _____	$	$	%
Credit card: _____	$	$	%
Total Credit Card Debt (Short-Term)	$	$	
Vehicle Loan 1 (include leases*)	$	$	%
Vehicle Loan 2 (include leases*)	$	$	%
Vehicle Loan 3	$	$	%
Bank Installment Loans	$	$	%
Student Loans	$	$	%
Total Consumer Debt (Intermediate-Term)	$	$	
First Mortgage	$	$	%
Second Mortgage	$	$	%
Total Long-Term Debt	$	$	
Total Owed and Total Monthly Payments	**$**	**$**	

*Leases are essentially a debt because you sign a contract that commits you to making payments for a certain period of time.

Step III: Reducing Debt
Do You Have Too Much?

1)   Add your Total Credit Card Debt payments to your Total Consumer Debt (in other words, don't include your mortgage) from the prior page and enter that amount here:
$_____

2)   Enter your take-home pay here: $_____. Divide your total from 1) above by your total take-home pay. This figure is the total of your consumer and credit card debts payments as a **percent of your disposable income**. For example, if your credit card payments are $200 a month and your car and student loan payments total $350 a month and your take-home pay is $2000 a month, your debt payments take up 28% percent of your disposable income. (Here's the math: $200 + $350 = $550 divided by $2000 = .28. In percentage terms, .28 is equal to 28%.) Here's what your number means to you:

Your Debt as a % of Disposable Income	Analysis	Take on Additional Debt?
10% or less	A safe limit; you feel little debt pressure	Be cautious
11-15%	Somewhat safe still; you feel some pressure	No
16-20%	You are fully extended; you probably can't handle an emergency without borrowing more	No – you're stepping over the edge
21-25%	You are overextended; you probably spend a lot of time worrying about how to make your payments	No – seek a financial counselor
26%+	You may feel desperate	No – you may need to declare bankruptcy unless you gain control of your debt

3)   Another approach for determining when debts are too large is **the continuous-debt method**. If you are unable to get completely out of debt every four years (except for mortgage and land contract loans), you probably lean on debt too heavily. You could be developing a credit lifestyle, in which you never eliminate debt and continuously pay out substantial amounts of income for finance charges, probably well over $1,000 a year.

Step IV: Create Your Plan to Reduce and Eliminate Debt

The best way to reduce and eliminate debt is to view your outstanding debt as one big amount, like a mortgage. When you make a mortgage (or rent) payment, you wouldn't dream of paying less than what was owed per month until the end of the term of the agreement for fear of losing the right to live in your home. Record your total debt "mortgage" from the information you entered in Step II on page 50 as follows:

Current Total Debt: $_____

Current Monthly Payment: $_____

You need to make the same commitment to eliminating debt as you do to paying your full monthly mortgage payment. You cannot reduce the amount you pay per month on your total outstanding debt until *all* your debt is paid off. (You have to decide whether this will include your mortgage – there are pros and cons to paying off your mortgage early. Consult a financial advisor or do more research to review this course of action.)

In order to prepare for your debt reduction and elimination program, you first need to do the following. It is similar to dieting – don't keep food in the house or elsewhere that might tempt you to veer from the program. Set up the following structure that will help you say "no" when the temptation to spend on credit arises.

- Pick one card to keep with a $5,000 maximum credit line for true emergencies.

- Cut up the rest of your credit cards, especially department store cards. Each department store takes VISA or MasterCard – there is no need for a separate card for each store. Don't be suckered into their "deals" of 10% off all your initial purchases if you open a credit card account. You'll spend 21% for the privilege of getting 10% off if you don't pay the entire amount right away! One card, one balance to manage, one payment. You need no more.

- Call each credit card company for the cards you will stop using and close that line of credit.

After 30-60 days, call the following credit bureaus to check your credit report to make sure the above actions are stated on your credit report. Expect to possibly pay a small fee to obtain a copy of the report (reports are around $8.50 per bureau), unless you have recently been denied credit (then the report is free). It is also a good idea to order these credit reports every 2-3 years to check for any errors. The main credit reporting agencies are as follows:
- *Experian - 888-397-3742 or on the Internet at www.experian.com*
- *Equifax Credit Information Services - 800-685-1111 or on the Internet at www.equifax.com*
- *Transunion – 800-916-8800 or on the Internet at www.tuc.com*

Step IV (cont'd): Create Your Plan to Reduce and Eliminate Debt

In order to get out of debt, you have to commit to one of the following methods:

1) *The Less Pain, Less Gain Method*: You cannot charge anything at all any more, or take on any new loans until you are debt free. Pay the minimum payments or what you're currently paying now every month if you can't afford to come up with extra money at this time. Once debts are paid off, re-assign those dollars towards the next highest interest debt on your list. Do not reduce the amount below what you are spending today on debt payments until **all** your debt is paid off. Close all accounts except for one you will use as needed and possibly one for emergencies (only if you don't have enough emergency savings set aside yet).

2) *The More Pain, More Gain Method*: You cannot charge anything at all any more, or take on any new loans until you are debt free. Cut your spending elsewhere and dig up an extra $50, $100 or $200 or more per month to accelerate your debt reduction. Add these additional funds to the payments for those credit lines with the highest interest rates. Once debts are paid off, re-assign those dollars towards the next highest interest debt on your list. Do not reduce the amount below what you are spending today on debt payments until all your debt is paid off. Close all accounts except for one you will use as needed and possibly one for emergencies (only if you don't have enough emergency savings set aside yet).

Stop Here
Record your answers on
your Action Plan on page 7
before moving on.

Investing Principle #1: Compounding

> Compounding is the principle of earning not only interest on the original money you saved, but earning interest on the interest.

Remember the twins Annie and Abbie from our example at the beginning of the book on the cost of procrastination? Annie (bottom, left) started saving for retirement at the age of 30, while Abbie waited and began at age 40. Annie put in $12,000 over six years and earned $39,000 at 10% interest on the $12,000 over 30 years. In addition, she earned $194,000 in *interest on the $39,000 of interest* since she started earlier. Abbie put in $50,000 of her own money and earned $ 65,000 at 10% on the $50,000 she had saved. But she only earned about $ 82,000 in *interest on the interest, or over $ 112,000 less than her sister, all because she started later.*

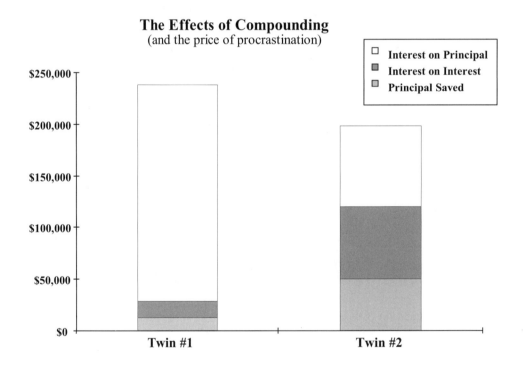

The Effects of Compounding
(and the price of procrastination)

Key:
- Interest on Principal
- Interest on Interest
- Principal Saved

Application:
How do you allow compounding to work for you?
Do you need a lot of money to use compounding?
What is the one thing you must do once you begin utilizing the principle of compounding?

Key: start now; no; do not take the money out.
You can change investments, but do not spend it.

The Risk of Possibly
Not Having Enough at Retirement
*Using Compounding to Become
an Investor Rather Than Just a Saver*

The following chart shows how the rate of return you earn affects the amount of benefit you receive from the principle of compounding. When saving for retirement, it behooves you to invest your money so you maximize the annual percent return you earn on your savings. The point is that just being a good saver is a start, but it isn't enough. *You have to also be a good investor.* Savers average 2-6% return on their investments since they are too afraid to take more risk. Investors accept more risk for the opportunity to earn higher average returns.

For example, on the table below, if you earned 6% on your $10,000 investment, in 20 years you would have only $32,071. If instead you earned 10% on average per year over those 20 years on your $10,000 investment, you would end up with $67,275. That's more than twice as much!

Compounded Annual Rate of Return on $10,000	6%	8%	10%	12%
Five years	$13,382	$14,693	$16,105	$17,623
Ten Years	$17,908	$21,589	$25,937	$31,058
Fifteen Years	$23,966	$31,722	$41,772	$54,736
Twenty Years	$32,071	$46,610	$67,275	$96,463

How can you apply the technique of combining compounding with higher rates of return to your own situation? Typically people fear something because they do not understand how it works. Learn more about investing in general to become familiar with the terminology. Learn as much as you can about the investments you have available to you through your employer-sponsored savings plans so you feel more comfortable using those that carry more risk. In addition, put to use the principle of dollar cost averaging and diversification that will be covered later in this chapter as a means of further decreasing risk and increasing returns. Pick one financial magazine to read every month so you are aware of what the investment markets are doing to help you increase your comfort with risk.

Setting Goals with Compounding

The following charts are to help you further apply the principle of compounding. Refer back to your goal sheet on page 41 and pick a goal to calculate how much you actually need to be saving today at a particular rate of return in order to reach that goal in the future.

Each of the following charts depicts a different situation. For example, you might have received $10,000 from the estate of a favorite aunt that recently passed away. What might that $10,000 grow to in the future if you invest it instead of buying a new car or paying down debt? Or, if your goal is to have $20,000 in 3 years for a down payment on a house, what might you need to be saving per month now to make that happen? Select the description below that most closely matches your situation and then fill in your numbers on that chart.

For Monthly Savings Plans:	*Chart To Use*
1) I know I can save $100 per month. What will my savings be worth in 10 years growing at 10%?	A
2) I want to have $15,000 saved in 5 years. How much should I save per month now if I can earn 6%?	B

One-Time Investments:

3) My boss paid me a one-time bonus check of $2,000. I am going to put it into a Roth IRA, and I will not be adding to it in the future. What will it be worth in 20 years if it grows at 12% per year?	C
4) I want to put aside a lump sum of money today for my son's future college education. What amount do I invest today at 8% in order to have $10,000 built up in 10 years?	D

Chart A - How Much Will My Monthly Savings Be Worth In The Future???

HOW TO USE THIS CHART:

	Your Numbers	Sample
1st: Multiply the monthly dollar amount you plan to save by 12 (to get your annual investment) and write the answer here:	$ _____	$100 x 12 = $ 1,200
2nd: Look at the interest rate/rate of return column you estimate you'll average and follow the column down to the number of years you want and write the "factor" here:	X 15.9374	X _____
3rd: Multiply the two numbers together, and your answer is how much your savings will be worth in the future!	$19,125	$ _____

SAVINGS FACTOR

No. of Yrs	6%	8%	10%	12%	15%	18%	20%
1	1.0000	1.0000	1.0000	1.0000	1.0000	1.0000	1.0000
2	2.0600	2.0800	2.1000	2.1200	2.1500	2.1800	2.2000
3	3.1836	3.2464	3.3100	3.3744	3.4725	3.5724	3.6400
4	4.3746	4.5061	4.6410	4.7793	4.9934	5.2154	5.3680
5	5.6371	5.8666	6.1051	6.3528	6.7424	7.1542	7.4416
6	6.9753	7.3359	7.7156	8.1152	8.7537	9.4420	9.9299
7	8.3938	8.9228	9.4872	10.0890	11.0668	12.1415	12.9159
8	9.8975	10.6366	11.4359	12.2997	13.7268	15.3270	16.4991
9	11.4913	12.4876	13.5795	14.7757	16.7858	19.0859	20.7989
10	13.1808	14.4866	15.9374	17.5487	20.3037	23.5213	25.9587
11	14.9716	16.6455	18.5312	20.6546	24.3493	28.7551	32.1504
12	16.8699	18.9771	21.3843	24.1331	29.0017	34.9311	39.5805
13	18.8821	21.4953	24.5227	28.0291	34.3519	42.2187	48.4966
14	21.0151	24.2149	27.9750	32.3926	40.5047	50.8180	59.1959
15	23.2760	27.1521	31.7725	37.2797	47.5804	60.9653	72.0351
16	25.6725	30.3243	35.9497	42.7533	55.7175	72.9390	87.4421
17	28.2129	33.7502	40.5447	48.8837	65.0751	87.0680	105.9306
18	30.9057	37.4502	45.5992	55.7497	75.8364	103.7403	128.1167
19	33.7600	41.4463	51.1591	63.4397	88.2118	123.4135	154.7400
20	36.7856	45.7620	57.2750	72.0524	102.4436	146.6280	186.6880
21	39.9927	50.4229	64.0025	81.6987	118.8101	174.0210	225.0256
22	43.3923	55.4568	71.4027	92.5026	137.6316	206.3448	271.0307
23	46.9958	60.8933	79.5430	104.6029	159.2764	244.4868	326.2369
24	50.8156	66.7648	88.4973	118.1552	184.1678	289.4945	392.4842
25	54.8645	73.1059	98.3471	133.3339	212.7930	342.6035	471.9811
26	59.1564	79.9544	109.1818	150.3339	245.7120	405.2721	567.3773
27	63.7058	87.3508	121.0999	169.3740	283.5688	479.2211	681.8528
28	68.5281	95.3388	134.2099	190.6989	327.1041	566.4809	819.2233
29	73.6398	103.9659	148.6309	214.5828	377.1697	669.4475	984.0680
30	79.0582	113.2832	164.4940	241.3327	434.7451	790.9480	1181.8816

Additional note: This is called a "Future Value of an Ordinary Annuity" chart with annual compounding. To be conservative, we use annual compounding instead of monthly compounding, even though we are figuring out how much a monthly amount will be in the future.

Chart B - How Much Do I Save Per Month Now If I Want A Certain Dollar Amount In The Future???

No. of Yrs	SAVINGS FACTOR						
	6%	8%	10%	12%	15%	18%	20%
1	1.0000	1.0000	1.0000	1.0000	1.0000	1.0000	1.0000
2	0.4854	0.4808	0.4762	0.4717	0.4651	0.4587	0.4545
3	0.3141	0.3080	0.3021	0.2963	0.2880	0.2799	0.2747
4	0.2286	0.2219	0.2155	0.2092	0.2003	0.1917	0.1863
5	0.1774	0.1705	0.1638	0.1574	0.1483	0.1398	0.1344
6	0.1434	0.1363	0.1296	0.1232	0.1142	0.1059	0.1007
7	0.1191	0.1121	0.1054	0.0991	0.0904	0.0824	0.0774
8	0.1010	0.0940	0.0874	0.0813	0.0729	0.0652	0.0606
9	0.0870	0.0801	0.0736	0.0677	0.0596	0.0524	0.0481
10	0.0759	0.0690	0.0627	0.0570	0.0493	0.0425	0.0385
11	0.0668	0.0601	0.0540	0.0484	0.0411	0.0348	0.0311
12	0.0593	0.0527	0.0468	0.0414	0.0345	0.0286	0.0253
13	0.0530	0.0465	0.0408	0.0357	0.0291	0.0237	0.0206
14	0.0476	0.0413	0.0357	0.0309	0.0247	0.0197	0.0169
15	0.0430	0.0368	0.0315	0.0268	0.0210	0.0164	0.0139
16	0.0390	0.0330	0.0278	0.0234	0.0179	0.0137	0.0114
17	0.0354	0.0296	0.0247	0.0205	0.0154	0.0115	0.0094
18	0.0324	0.0267	0.0219	0.0179	0.0132	0.0096	0.0078
19	0.0296	0.0241	0.0195	0.0158	0.0113	0.0081	0.0065
20	0.0272	0.0219	0.0175	0.0139	0.0098	0.0068	0.0054
21	0.0250	0.0198	0.0156	0.0122	0.0084	0.0057	0.0044
22	0.0230	0.0180	0.0140	0.0108	0.0073	0.0048	0.0037
23	0.0213	0.0164	0.0126	0.0096	0.0063	0.0041	0.0031
24	0.0197	0.0150	0.0113	0.0085	0.0054	0.0035	0.0025
25	0.0182	0.0137	0.0102	0.0075	0.0047	0.0029	0.0021
26	0.0169	0.0125	0.0092	0.0067	0.0041	0.0025	0.0018
27	0.0157	0.0114	0.0083	0.0059	0.0035	0.0021	0.0015
28	0.0146	0.0105	0.0075	0.0052	0.0031	0.0018	0.0012
29	0.0136	0.0096	0.0067	0.0047	0.0027	0.0015	0.0010
30	0.0126	0.0088	0.0061	0.0041	0.0023	0.0013	0.0008

HOW TO USE THIS CHART:

Your Numbers / Sample

1st: Write the value of the dollar amount you want to have in the future here:

Sample: $ 15,000

Your Numbers: $ _____

2nd: Look at the interest rate/rate of return column you estimate you'll average and follow the column down to the number of years you want and write the factor here:

Sample: 6% For For 5 yrs

X 0.1774 X _____

3rd: Multiply the two numbers together, and your answer is how much you need to save per year now to reach your goal.

Sample: $ 2,661

$ _____

4th: Divide step 3 (your annual amount) by 12, and your answer is how much you need to save per month to reach your goal!

Sample: Step 3 divided by 12 = $221.75/mo

Step 3 divided by 12 = $ _____

Additional note: This is called the "Present Value of an Ordinary Annuity" chart with annual compounding. To be conservative, we use annual compounding instead of monthly compounding, even though we are figuring out how much to save monthly.

© Copyright 1990-2005, Discover Learning, Inc.

Chart C - How Much Will My One-Time Investment Be Worth in the Future??

HOW TO USE THIS CHART:

1st: Write the dollar amount of your one-time investment here:

Sample $ 2,000 $ _____

2nd: Look at the interest rate/rate of return column you estimate you'll average and follow the column down to the number of years you want and write the factor here:

X 9.6463 X _____

3rd: Multiply the two numbers together and your answer is how much your savings will be worth in the future!

$ 19,293 $ _____

Additional note: This is called a "Future Value of a Lump Sum" chart with annual compounding.

No. of Yrs	SAVINGS FACTOR						
	6%	8%	10%	12%	15%	18%	20%
1	1.0600	1.0800	1.1000	1.1200	1.1500	1.1800	1.2000
2	1.1236	1.1664	1.2100	1.2544	1.3225	1.3924	1.4400
3	1.1910	1.2597	1.3310	1.4049	1.5209	1.6430	1.7280
4	1.2625	1.3605	1.4641	1.5735	1.7490	1.9388	2.0736
5	1.3382	1.4693	1.6105	1.7623	2.0114	2.2878	2.4883
6	1.4185	1.5869	1.7716	1.9738	2.3131	2.6996	2.9860
7	1.5036	1.7138	1.9487	2.2107	2.6600	3.1855	3.5832
8	1.5938	1.8509	2.1436	2.4760	3.0590	3.7589	4.2998
9	1.6895	1.9990	2.3579	2.7731	3.5179	4.4355	5.1598
10	1.7908	2.1589	2.5937	3.1058	4.0456	5.2338	6.1917
11	1.8983	2.3316	2.8531	3.4785	4.6524	6.1759	7.4301
12	2.0122	2.5182	3.1384	3.8960	5.3503	7.2876	8.9161
13	2.1329	2.7196	3.4523	4.3635	6.1528	8.5994	10.6993
14	2.2609	2.9372	3.7975	4.8871	7.0757	10.1472	12.8392
15	2.3966	3.1722	4.1772	5.4736	8.1371	11.9737	15.4070
16	2.5404	3.4259	4.5950	6.1304	9.3576	14.1290	18.4884
17	2.6928	3.7000	5.0545	6.8660	10.7613	16.6722	22.1861
18	2.8543	3.9960	5.5599	7.6900	12.3755	19.6733	26.6233
19	3.0256	4.3157	6.1159	8.6128	14.2318	23.2144	31.9480
20	3.2071	4.6610	6.7275	**9.6463**	16.3665	27.3930	38.3376
21	3.3996	5.0338	7.4002	10.8038	18.8215	32.3238	46.0051
22	3.6035	5.4365	8.1403	12.1003	21.6447	38.1421	55.2061
23	3.8197	5.8715	8.9543	13.5523	24.8915	45.0076	66.2474
24	4.0489	6.3412	9.8497	15.1786	28.6252	53.1090	79.4968
25	4.2919	6.8485	10.8347	17.0001	32.9190	62.6686	95.3962
26	4.5494	7.3964	11.9182	19.0401	37.8568	73.9490	114.4755
27	4.8223	7.9881	13.1100	21.3249	43.5353	87.2598	137.3706
28	5.1117	8.6271	14.4210	23.8839	50.0656	102.9666	164.8447
29	5.4184	9.3173	15.8631	26.7499	57.5755	121.5005	197.8136
30	5.7435	10.0627	17.4494	29.9599	66.2118	143.3706	237.3763

Chart D - How Much of a One-Time Investment Do I Put Aside Now to Have a Certain Amount in the Future?

HOW TO USE THIS CHART:

	Sample	Your Numbers
1st: Write the value of the dollar amount you want to have in the future here:	$ 10,000	$ _____
2nd: Look at the interest rate/rate of return column you estimate you'll average and follow the column down to the number of years you want and write the "factor" here:	X .4632	X _____
3rd: Multiply the two numbers together, and your answer is how much you need to set aside now to reach your goal!	$ 4,632	$ _____

No. of Yrs	SAVINGS FACTOR						
	6%	8%	10%	12%	15%	18%	20%
1	0.9434	0.9259	0.9091	0.8929	0.8696	0.8475	0.8333
2	0.8900	0.8573	0.8264	0.7972	0.7561	0.7182	0.6944
3	0.8396	0.7938	0.7513	0.7118	0.6575	0.6086	0.5787
4	0.7921	0.7350	0.6830	0.6355	0.5718	0.5158	0.4823
5	0.7473	0.6806	0.6209	0.5674	0.4972	0.4371	0.4019
6	0.7050	0.6302	0.5645	0.5066	0.4323	0.3704	0.3349
7	0.6651	0.5835	0.5132	0.4523	0.3759	0.3139	0.2791
8	0.6274	0.5403	0.4665	0.4039	0.3269	0.2660	0.2326
9	0.5919	0.5002	0.4241	0.3606	0.2843	0.2255	0.1938
10	0.5584	**0.4632**	0.3855	0.3220	0.2472	0.1911	0.1615
11	0.5268	0.4289	0.3505	0.2875	0.2149	0.1619	0.1346
12	0.4970	0.3971	0.3186	0.2567	0.1869	0.1372	0.1122
13	0.4688	0.3677	0.2897	0.2292	0.1625	0.1163	0.0935
14	0.4423	0.3405	0.2633	0.2046	0.1413	0.0985	0.0779
15	0.4173	0.3152	0.2394	0.1827	0.1229	0.0835	0.0649
16	0.3936	0.2919	0.2176	0.1631	0.1069	0.0708	0.0541
17	0.3714	0.2703	0.1978	0.1456	0.0929	0.0600	0.0451
18	0.3503	0.2502	0.1799	0.1300	0.0808	0.0508	0.0376
19	0.3305	0.2317	0.1635	0.1161	0.0703	0.0431	0.0313
20	0.3118	0.2145	0.1486	0.1037	0.0611	0.0365	0.0261
21	0.2942	0.1987	0.1351	0.0926	0.0531	0.0309	0.0217
22	0.2775	0.1839	0.1228	0.0826	0.0462	0.0262	0.0181
23	0.2618	0.1703	0.1117	0.0738	0.0402	0.0222	0.0151
24	0.2470	0.1577	0.1015	0.0659	0.0349	0.0188	0.0126
25	0.2330	0.1460	0.0923	0.0588	0.0304	0.0160	0.0105
26	0.2198	0.1352	0.0839	0.0525	0.0264	0.0135	0.0087
27	0.2074	0.1252	0.0763	0.0469	0.0230	0.0115	0.0073
28	0.1956	0.1159	0.0693	0.0419	0.0200	0.0097	0.0061
29	0.1846	0.1073	0.0630	0.0374	0.0174	0.0082	0.0051
30	0.1741	0.0994	0.0573	0.0334	0.0151	0.0070	0.0042

Additional note: This is called a "Present Value of a Future Sum" chart with annual compounding.

Investing Principle #2: Diversification

> Diversification is the principle of spreading your assets around, or not putting all your eggs in one basket.

Let's say you have $50,000 in your employer-sponsored retirement saving account and that you have been primarily using one of the investment options available to you, namely a conservative guaranteed interest contract or a government bond fund. You have two options: you can continue doing what you've been doing (i.e., earning 4% a year), or you can "take more risk" and divide your money up between five of the other investments available to you.

Option #1:

$50,000 @ 4% for 25 yrs. = $ 133,292 after 25 years

-OR-

Option #2:

$10,000 @ 2% for 25 yrs. = $ 16,406
$10,000 @ 4% for 25 yrs. = $ 26,658
$10,000 @ 6% for 25 yrs. = $ 42,919
$10,000 @ 8% for 25 yrs. = $ 68,485
$10,000 @ 10% for 25 yrs. = $ 108,347

$ 262,815 after 25 years

The benefits of diversifying to you are that you:

- _____ *your overall rate of return.*

- _____ *your overall risk.*

- *Get better protection from* _____.

Key: increase, decrease, inflation

Diversification and Asset Classes

There are different types of investments. For some, their purpose is to grow in value (i.e., equities or common stocks). For others their purpose is to produce income, with little potential for growth in value (i.e., bonds, certificates of deposits). The chart below shows what has happened historically when you *diversify* or spread your money into both types of investments.

If You Own:	Your Average Return*:	The Single Largest One-Year Gain:	The Single Largest One-Year Loss:
80% stocks/20% bonds	12.2%	43.5%	(20.3%)
60% stocks/40% bonds	10.7%	34.4%	(14.1%)
50% stocks/50% bonds	10.0%	31.6%	(11.1%)
40% stocks/60% bonds	9.3%	32.8%	(8.0%)
20% stocks/80% bonds	7.8%	36.6%	(6.0%)

What does this mean to you? If you look at the far right column, you can see that money was lost in the past when that particular combination of stocks and bonds were used. Two points to be made here are:

1) There is risk in every investment you use, and
2) The different combinations produced different average rates of return.

The investing **Rule of 72** says by taking the number 72 and dividing it by the expected rate of return, you will come up with the number of years it will take to double your money. For example, if you decided to use a combination of 80% stocks and 20% bonds in the past, you would have doubled your money every 5.9 years (72 divided by 12.2 = 5.9 years). But if you had used the opposite 20% stock and 80% bond asset allocation, you would only have doubled your money every 9.2 years (72 divided by 7.8 = 9.2 years).

Take a moment and pull out one of your investment statements. Find the rate of return you are earning and divide 72 by that rate of return. How long will it take you to double your money? Are you satisfied with that? Will it be sufficient for meeting your goals? If you are late getting started in saving for retirement, you may have to combine your investments in a way that produces higher returns for the increased risk, or extend the time you plan on working prior to retirement.

*1950 through 2003, compounded annually, dividends reinvested. **Source: © *Stocks, Bonds, Bills and Inflation* 2003 Yearbook™,** Ibbotson Associates, Chicago (annually updates work by Roger G. Ibbotson and Rex A. Sinquefield). Used with permission. All rights reserved.

Investing Principle #3:
Dollar Cost Averaging

> *"Dollar Cost Averaging" is a system of automatically buying more shares when prices are lower, and fewer shares when prices are higher, by investing fixed dollar amounts at regular intervals.*

What do you do when a consumer item that you use regularly goes on sale? You stock up and buy more! Why? Because you know you are lowering your per unit cost. Investing works the same way. If we use the principle of dollar cost averaging, our money automatically goes farther for us. Should we be worried if the value of our investments temporarily goes down? If we are a long term investor (i.e., when you do not need the money you have saved during the next five years), no! We should instead be happy, since the money that is going into our savings is now able to buy <u>more</u> for our money. Here's an example:

Example: The Paper Towel Sale	Fixed Amount "Invested"	Price Per Item	Number of Items Purchased
Week #1: Regular Price	$10	1.17	8.5
Week #2: Semi-Sale Week!	$10	0.89	11.2
Week #3: Super Sale Week!!	$10	0.59	16.9
Week #4: Regular Price	<u>$10</u>	<u>1.17</u>	<u>8.5</u>
Total dollars	$40		45 units (approximately)

Average price/item over 4 weeks $ 0.96

Average price actually paid ($40 spent divided by 45 items purchased) $ 0.89

Why was the per unit price we actually paid (89¢) for the paper towels less than what the store actually offered as a price on average (96¢)? *Because we bought more units when the prices were lower, and therefore it lowered our overall average cost.* The same thing works with your investments. Dollar cost averaging relieves you from guessing when the market will go "on sale," and allows you to automatically benefit from lower prices when it does. Dollar cost averaging:

- Relieves you from _____ your investments.
- Helps overcome _____.
- Works easily into a _____.
- Creates the _____ of (forced) saving and investing.

Key: timing, procrastination, spending plan, habit

How to Confidently
Accomplish Your Goals
Summary

Substantial wealth can be built by:

- Saving the maximum amount every year that your employer-sponsored retirement plan will allow.

- Using debt intelligently and being committed to paying it off early. Then use some or all of those dollars to put into your retirement savings account.

- Using time and compounding to do the bulk of the work so you're not trading hours for dollars all your life. Save on a regular basis (weekly or monthly) over a long period of time by using payroll deduction plans through work or credit unions, 401(k), or other retirement savings plans, etc.

- Protecting your money from wealth robbers - inflation, taxes, lack of diversification, improper insurance coverage, interest charges, etc.

- Diversifying your money, with at least one-third to one-half in investments that provide growth no matter what your age. Shoot for rates of return that are above the combined rates of inflation and taxes.

Stop Here

Record your answers on
your Action Plan on page 7
before moving on.

Home:
Implement Your Plan

Step I: Why Use a Spending Plan (a/k/a a Budget)?

Here's where we dig up dollars to help fund your goals.

Why use a budget, or in other words, plan your spending?
Studies have shown that many millionaires are ordinary people who work and save regularly like the rest of us. However, they know exactly how much their family spends in each and every household expenditure category. A spending plan is the primary tool they use to help them control their expenses and achieve financial freedom.

Why do we call it a "spending plan" instead of a "budget"? For many, the word "budget" denotes sacrifice, denial of quality of life, and hints at deprivation. For these reasons, budgets do not inspire many people to want to use one! In reality, the underlying purpose of a budget is to provide a road map of how you have chosen to spend your money. Thus use of a "spending plan" allows you to be in control by providing a roadmap to refer to on a weekly basis so the dollars you earn are properly allocated to uses you have pre-determined.

If you're the type who worries about money, it probably stems from the uncertainty of being able to pay bills. A budget allows you to work all your numbers ahead of time on paper. If it looks like you will have a shortfall, then plan to cut your spending in other areas until your inflow equals your anticipated outflow. It's a lot easier to have anxiety and sweaty palms about money once a month when you plan your budget instead of every time you try to charge something and aren't sure if your card will be accepted! Use that negative energy positively instead over the rest of the month by doing something about changing your financial situation.

Studies have also shown there is an inverse relationship between the time spent purchasing luxury items such as cars and clothes, or watching football or the week's prime time lineup, and the time spent planning one's financial future. Make a commitment to yourself and your family to invest eight (8) hours a month in planning your financial future through the use of a spending plan. Only one short evening a week or a two-hour investment on the weekend for three months will provide the structure you need to balance planning, investing and consuming your household's income.

Once you get your system down, you will actually spend less time on money matters since you have planned in advance the outcomes you seek. Do you remember the first time you drove a car? You were so aware of keeping your hands at ten and two on the steering wheel, of making sure traffic was clear before changing lanes, etc. After awhile it was second nature. It didn't take much effort at all! The same will happen as you create and begin using your budget. It may seem strange at first and take a lot of thought, but soon it will get easier and easier!

As you take charge of your financial future through this most important tool, you will find many other areas of your life will also improve. Communication with your spouse, significant other, children, friends or co-workers will be more open, productive, and less stressed. In addition, you will become more relaxed and have more time available to pay attention to other things in life besides putting out financial fires! You'll sleep better at night, and be more confident about your life in general. In short, soon you will regain the two hours a week you've invested in your spending plan since you will spend less time trying to make ends meet.

In order to get the most from this program and your new spending plan, we recommend you complete the net worth, goal setting, retirement planning, college funding and debt reduction sections before beginning creating your budget.

Here's what we'll cover in this section:

Step 1: Why use a budget?

Step 2: Where is your money going *now*?

Step 3: Where do you *want* your money to go each month?
(Create your average monthly budget and include your goals!)

Step 4: Compare your budget to what you actually spent. How close did you come?

Happy budgeting!

Step II:
Where is Your
Money Going Now?

Use the monthly expense tracking form on the next page to further help you collect information about your current spending. This is especially helpful if you're in the habit of running to an ATM machine every time you need cash. Have you ever thought to yourself, "Where did all that money go?" You remember taking the money out of your account but have little to no recollection of where it went!

Commit to tracking your spending by investing 2-3 minutes at the end of the day for the next two to three months in addition to filling out the three-page spending plan form so you make sure your budget truly reflects your spending. To make your numbers even more complete, ask your spouse or significant other to do the same if you will work on managing your spending together.

Variable Spending Tracking Sheet

For the month: _____

Instructions for tracking your variable spending:

1) Set up spending item categories in the far left "Item" column in the same order as shown on your spending plan form.

2) Every evening, record (in pencil) the cash you spent that day (cash only; checks written will be done later).

3) At the end of every month, review your checkbook and fill in what you spent on various days in the various spending categories.

4) Then, total the rows for each spending category and compare to what was budgeted; make adjustments on your spending plan for the future as needed.

ITEM	1	2	3	4	5	6	7	8	9	10	11	12	13	14	15	16	17	18	19	20	21	22	23	24	25	26	27	28	29	30	31	TOTALS
Gas																																
Snacks																																
Coffee																																
Magazine																																
Newspprs																																
Cigarette																																
Car Wash																																
Eat Out																																
Movies																																

69

Where is Your
Money Going Now?

Once you're ready to begin creating your budget, pull out your pay stubs, checkbooks, credit card statements, bank statements and your monthly tracking sheets for the last three months to pull together the information you'll need for the next few pages. In the following worksheets you will be collecting information in four areas. The more detail you can provide in each section will allow you a greater level of control. These four areas are:

1. **Current income.**
2. **Fixed expenses.** Added to your fixed variable expenses, they should account for no more than 70% of your total monthly after-tax income. Monthly fixed expenses are obligations where the dollars paid stay the same month after month.
3. **Fixed variable expenses** are obligations where the amount paid per month may vary within a certain range.
4. **Variable expenses** are those that vary from month to month. Whenever you're running short of funds, this is the first place to look since these expenses can temporarily be cut back or cut out if needed.

Current Income

Take a few moments to collect the following information. Once finished, transfer your data to the first page of your spending plan on page 75.

Sources of Income	Current Average Monthly Income
Partner A (after-tax)	
Partner B (after-tax)	
Bonuses/Commission	
Interest/Dividends	
Rents/Royalties	
Other _____	
Other _____	
Other _____	
TOTAL INCOME BY MONTH	

Monthly Fixed Expenses

Monthly fixed expenses are obligations where the dollars paid stay the same month after month. Added to the fixed variable expenses on the next page, they should account for no more than 70% of your total monthly after-tax income.

Fixed Expenses	Monthly Average
401(k)/Retirement Savings	$
Other Savings	
Mortgage/Rent Payment	
Second Mortgage Payment	
Real Estate Taxes	
Car Payment - 1	
Car Payment - 2	
Other Loans - 1	
Other Loans - 2	
Other Loans - 3	
Life Insurance	
Medical Insurance	
Disability Insurance	
Auto Insurance	
Homeowners/Renters Insurance	
Alimony	
Child Support	
Clubs/Dues	
Goal - 1 _____	
Goal - 2 _____	
Goal - 3 _____	
Other	

Monthly Fixed Variable Expenses

Fixed variable amounts are obligations where the amount paid per month may vary within a certain range.

Fixed Variable Amounts	Monthly Average
Electricity	$
Heating Fuel/Gas	
Water	
Garbage Pickup	
Telephone	
Cable/satellite TV	
Auto Expense/Gas	
Other Transportation (parking, bus, etc.)	
Church Charity Contributions	
Credit Card Debt - 1 _____	
Credit Card Debt - 2 _____	
Credit Card Debt - 3 _____	
Credit Card Debt - 4 _____	
Credit Card Debt - 5 _____	
Other	

Variable Expenses

Variable expenses are those that vary from month to month. Whenever you're running short of funds, this is the first place to look since these expenses can usually be temporarily cut back, delayed, or cut out if needed.

Variable Expenses	Monthly Average
Spending/Pocket Money	$
Groceries	
Childcare	
School	
Personal Hygiene Products	
Cleaners	
House Cleaning	
Haircuts/Nails/Beauty Salon	
Medical	
Dental	
Auto Repairs	
Home Repairs/Maintenance	
Clothing	
Vacations	
Entertainment, gifts	
Sports	
Magazine/Newspapers/Books	
Miscellaneous	

Step III:
Where Do You Want Your Money to Go?

In this section you will transfer the information you collected on the prior pages onto the actual Spending Plan form. There is an extra copy of the Spending Plan form in Appendix A so you can make copies. The goal of your Spending Plan should be to plan to spend less or equal to the amount you take home every month. Consult the sample in Appendix B.

USING A PENCIL, start with just the Projected Average Column first:

1. In the row at the top, write in the first letter of the month you are beginning with under the numbers '1', '2', '3', etc. For example, if the next month is February, put a 'F' in the box '1'. Add 'M' to '2' for March, and so on. This way you can customize the form to begin when you want it to. You can use it for just part of the year, and then when the New Year comes, begin a new form with the first month as January.

2. Enter your monthly income in the Projected Average Column.

3. Referring to your goal sheet on page 41, write in your top three goals. Put at least one of them on the "Fixed Costs" page. Use the '#' column to remind you of the number or priority of the goal, i.e., 1, 2, 3 etc.

4. Referring back to the prior pages where you collected information on your current spending on pages 69-73, and using the charts across from the Spending Plan form pages, write in *only* those expense categories that reflect your monthly costs. Again, this way you customize the form to your specific needs.

5. Put a checkmark in the '*' column if you need to set up a separate account to collect money to meet a periodic expense like Christmas, car insurance, tuition, or summer and winter property taxes. Write it on your Action Plan to set up those accounts and have money transferred over monthly.

6. Fill in the dollar amounts you estimate you'll average per month for each category. Use the tables across from the Spending Plan pages for ideas on ways to cut back or cut out expenses.

7. Total your monthly income estimate, and then your monthly expenses. If your total expenses are greater than your total monthly income, get your pencil and eraser out and hunt for ways to cut back. It is most likely that your goals are throwing you over budget since most people find they were not spending money in the past on their goals. It's time to dig up dollars!

8. Go back and repeat Steps Two and Five for each of the 12 months. Remember to reallocate dollars freed up from goals that have been accomplished to your next highest goal. In addition, once a debt is paid off, reallocate those dollars toward the next highest interest rate debt in order to pay off debts rapidly!

Twelve Month Spending Plan

As of: _____

SOURCES OF INCOME	PROJECTED (AVERAGE)	1	2	3	4	5	6	7	8	9	10	11	12	12 MONTH TOTAL
Partner A (after-tax)														
Partner B (after-tax)														
Bonuses/Commission														
Interest/Dividends														
Rents/Royalties														
Other _____														
Other _____														
Other _____														
A. TOTAL INCOME BY MONTH														
Subtract Anticipated Monthly Expenses														
CASH AVAILABLE/ CASH NEEDED ±														

Planned Expenditures For the Month			
B. Actual Expenditures For the Month			
Amount Under ( ) or Over + (A − B)			

If in case you would prefer to further customize or more specifically define your spending categories, circle additional items on the following tables. Enter their name and estimated amount on the spending plan form in the column named "Projected Average" on the next page, along with the personal data you collected on page 71.

Common Fixed and Periodic Expense Categories

Fixed Expenses	*Periodic Expenses*
• Alimony	• Income taxes
• Boat loans	• Disability insurance
• Car (gas, parking, tires, insurance, etc.)	• Safety deposit box
• Child support	• Post office box
• Credit card debt	• Property taxes
• Day care	• Homeowner's insurance
• Education	• Renter's insurance
• Electricity	• Christmas
• Gas (heating)	• Seasonal dues
• Medical insurance	• Water bill
• Rent/mortgage	• Trash pickup
• Land contract payments	• Miscellaneous
• Student loan(s)	• Other
• Telephone	
• Union dues	
• Miscellaneous	
• Other	

Ways To Cut Or Eliminate Fixed Costs

If your numbers aren't adding up, consider using some of the following ways to dig up dollars from your fixed expenses:

- Examine insurance policies for potential lost savings, i.e., raise the deductible on your car from $250 to $500.
- Refinance debt to a lower cost loan such as a home equity loan.
- Be conservative with the use of utilities.
- Participate in retirement savings programs which then reduce taxes.
- Cancel unnecessary insurance, i.e., children's life insurance.
- Avoid using credit cards - pay cash.
- Sell big items that you don't use much, i.e., boat, snowmobile, etc.

CATEGORY	*	PROJ AVG	#	1	2	3	4	5	6	7	8	9	10	11	12	12 MONTH TOTAL
FIXED COSTS:																
Goal																
Goal																
Goal																
PERIODIC COSTS:																
TOTAL FIXED & PERIODIC COSTS																

Home: Implement Your Plan

If in case you would prefer to further customize or more specifically define your spending categories, circle additional items on the following tables. Enter their name and estimated amount on the spending plan form in the column named "Projected Average" on the next page, along with the personal data you collected on pages 72 to 73.

Common Variable Expense Categories

• Books	• Home furnishings
• Charitable contributions	• Home repairs
• Children's expenses	• Home supplies
• Clothing cosmetics	• Housecleaning
• Eating out	• Investments
• Dry cleaning	• Laundry
• Education	• Legal expenses
• Entertainment (movies, theater, concerts, etc.)	• Magazines/newspaper
• Gifts	• Medical expenses
• Groceries	• Personal care
• Haircuts/beauty salon	• Personal growth (seminars, therapy, etc.)
• Health club	• Professional growth
• Hobby	• Sports
• Home equipment (small appliances, kitchen equipment and tools)	• Vacations
	• Miscellaneous
	• Other

Ways To Cut Or Eliminate Variable Costs

If your numbers aren't adding up, consider using some of the following ways to dig up dollars by cutting variable costs:

- Cut down on pleasure spending (buy one C.D. a month instead of four).
- Eat at home more often; shop for groceries after a meal.
- Buy in bulk and at discount stores.
- Make a list before you shop and stick to it.
- Do repairs and maintenance yourself.
- Use coupons.
- Buy generic goods.
- Buy used furniture and autos.
- Buy clothing, toys, etc. secondhand at garage sales, estate auctions and thrift shops.
- Cut out spending on goods or services that hold no value to you.
- Limit the number of evenings and/or lunches when you go out.

CATEGORY	*	PROJ AVG	#	1	2	3	4	5	6	7	8	9	10	11	12	12 MO. TOTAL
VARIABLE COSTS:																
Goal																
Goal																
Goal																
TOTAL VARIABLE COSTS																

DEBT TRACKING	#	1	2	3	4	5	6	7	8	9	10	11	12	BAL.

Step IV: Using Your Spending Plan

After you have constructed your spending plan:

1) _____ it.

- Whether you use mostly cash or checks is a personal choice, but record any expenditure over one dollar.
- If you charge an item, record that expense at its full expense (even though you will be paying for it over time) unless it is a durable item such as a major appliance.
- Do not use charge cards for expendable items, since they distort your view of how well you live within your monthly income.

2) _____ your new spending behavior to the amounts you allocated for each spending category.

If you experience a large gap between what you spent and what you allocated then:

- You might have been too drastic, i.e., cutting your food budget to $100 per month. This will make you miserable and will bust your budget.
- The item might be seasonal and you are experiencing the "peak" season, i.e., heating bills, clothes, etc. View these items in context with their overall yearly cost.
- You may be becoming lazy and falling back into old habits instead of working toward your new goals.

3) _____ !!! What to do when unexpected expenses arise, such as the car breaks down, the roof leaks, etc.

- Analyze your current spending plan for places you can cut back for several months (i.e., essential vs. nice items) so you don't deplete savings and avoid increasing debt.
- Use your emergency savings. That's what it's there for. Set up a plan to replenish your savings over the next several months.
- Utilize debt as a last resort. Set up a plan to pay it off within three to twelve months.

Key: analyze, compare, surprise

Average Household Spending:
Fixed Costs

	Less Than 25	Age of Householder				
		25 - 34	35 - 44	45 - 54	55 - 64	65 or Older
Median Annual Household Income . . (Before taxes)	$20,680	$50,389	$61,091	$68,028	$58,672	$30,437
Median Monthly Household Income . . (Before taxes)	$1,723	$4,199	$5,091	$5,669	$4,889	$2,536
Average Monthly Expenditures of certain Fixed Costs:						
Housing	591	1,199	1,342	1,302	1,143	811
Utilities	111	215	262	278	257	207
Transportation	390	676	741	814	723	402
Health Care	46	122	175	207	255	312
Personal Insurance and Pensions	115	345	433	500	402	104
Taxes	35	165	235	329	236	157

Source: The 2003 Consumer Expenditure Survey, Bureau of Labor Statistics

Average Household Spending:
Variable Costs

	Less Than 25	25 - 34	35 - 44	45 - 54	55 - 64	65 or Older
			Age of Householder			
Median Annual Household Income . . (Before taxes)	$20,680	$50,389	$61,091	$68,028	$58,672	$30,437
Median Monthly Household Income . . (Before taxes)	$1,723	$4,199	$5,091	$5,669	$4,889	$2,536
Average Monthly Expenditures of certain Variable Costs:						
Food at Home	147	248	300	308	276	215
Eating Out	136	195	223	224	185	110
Entertainment	79	163	210	201	201	122
Clothing	93	154	174	163	130	76
Education	124	57	58	115	62	11
Household Furnishings and Equipment	61	131	144	150	153	77
Alcoholic Beverages	42	37	35	40	31	15
Total Average Monthly Expenditures	**$1,866**	**$3,377**	**$3,931**	**$4,175**	**$3,683**	**$2,448**

Source: The 2003 Consumer Expenditure Survey, Bureau of Labor Statistics

Spending Plan Summary

Out of everything included in this workbook (including the Action Plan), your Spending Plan is THE most important tool.

Why?

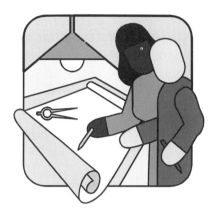

Because it is here where you actually *implement* on a monthly basis all you have uncovered, discovered and planned for during the course of this book. In essence, your Spending Plan is the specific blueprint or instructions you have created for how you are going to achieve your financial and personal goals.

Take a moment right now and write on your Action Plan a commitment to investing in a two-hour weekly session to create and implement your personalized Spending Plan over the next several weeks.   I guarantee the results will be striking!

By doing so, you will:
- Be in more control
- Be able to more fully enjoy your relationships with your family, friends and co-workers
- Create a proven, easy to use and meaningful system to accomplish your goals
- Have readily available the information needed to make more informed financial decisions.

In the future, consult your Spending Plan before making new financial commitments. It's difficult to remember what you wrote down, decided on, or agreed to in your Spending Plan when there is a strong urge to upgrade your car or get new furniture at 50% off with 0% financing in a year-end clearance sale! Once you learn to say 'NO" to unplanned expenditures, and say 'YES' to sticking with what you have already planned, you will truly experience the secret to successfully controlling your financial future.

<u>*Stop Here*</u>
Record your answers on
your Action Plan on page 7
before moving on.

Workbook Summary

Several years ago there was a young woman who attended one of our "Controlling Your Financial Future" workshops through her employer. She was a single mom, living in a two-bedroom apartment with two young children, trying to make ends meet. She attended the workshop to help her find a way to purchase a home for her family so her kids could have their own rooms and a backyard to play in. By chance, we ran into her three years later. She was all excited and just beamed as she thanked us for the course and what she had learned in it. Because of it, and how she applied what she learned, she was able to purchase a cozy, three-bedroom bungalow where her kids had their own room and a nice backyard to play in.

People changing, improving and gaining control of their lives. People improving their relationships, experiencing less stress and increased peace of mind. All done through better financial management knowledge and skills. For us, that's what it's all about.

During this workbook we have:
- Reviewed your financial foundation (insurance, estate plan)
- Created a net worth statement
- Set values-based goals
- Planned to reduce and eliminate debt
- Discovered powerful and easy-to-use wealth building techniques
- Created a personalized Spending Plan that incorporates all the above
- Created an Action Plan to help you implement your plan.

We encourage you to establish the habit of investing two hours a week in controlling your financial future. *The years go by so quickly.* With every New Year comes reminiscing about how quickly the prior year flew by. Another year gone without financial action means the cost of your goals will go up. However, once set up, your financial plan can go on autopilot and keep on working while you focus on other aspects of life. Mini-checkups made three or four times a year are all you then need to make sure you're still on course.

We believe that every individual is capable of creating and implementing a basic financial plan when they are taught a system to follow and are provided with the proper environment in which to learn. The material here is the basis for all financial planning. Many of you, though, might still need the help of a financial professional since your needs might go beyond the scope of this book. When you enlist their help, take this book and any current worksheets with you in order to save you time and money.

We truly hope you feel the time you have invested in completing this workbook will help you experience greater confidence, knowledge and peace of when making financial decisions. Thank you for the opportunity to be of service. When you get a chance, please drop us a line and let us know how you're doing!

Appendix A:
Annual Update System

At the end of each section of this book, we will stop and direct you to record your Action Ideas on this Action Plan. When you have completed the workbook, tear this page out and post it on your refrigerator, your bathroom mirror, or keep it with your monthly bills as a reminder to complete the actions you have determined during the program.

My Action Plan

Determine Where You Are

Quick Check Financial Assessment (page 11)

Actions I Need To Take	**Target Date**
1) _____	_____
2) _____	_____
3) _____	_____
4) _____	_____
5) _____	_____

Net Worth Actions to Take (page 29)

My Net Worth Isn't As Strong As It Could Be Because: *Ways to Strengthen My Net Worth:*

_____

_____

_____

With my next raise I will: _____

With my next windfall I will: _____

Determine Where You Want to Go

Values-Based Goal Setting:

In the next one to three years, it is very important to me that I accomplish the following goals (page 41):

	Goal	Total Amount Needed	Amount Needed Per Month
1)	_____	_____	_____
2)	_____	_____	_____
3)	_____	_____	_____

How to Confidently Accomplish Your Goals

Wealth-building techniques that I will use to help me meet my goals (pages 45 to 64):

	Technique	Application	Goal
Example:	Debt Reduction	Consolidate Debt	Eliminate Credit Card Debt
1)	_____	_____	_____
2)	_____	_____	_____
3)	_____	_____	_____

Implement Your Plan

From the spending plan worksheets on pages 75 to 79:

I can find $_____ per month to apply towards my goals.

I will begin using my spending plan as of _____ (month & year).

Your Annual Checkup System

Once a year, invest the time to go through the following steps to maintain your financial plan and control your financial future:

A)   Update your net worth and debt repayment statements.

B)   Compare where you are now versus where you were last year using the net worth and debt graphs.

C)   Review the status of your emergency savings*.

D)   Review your insurance coverage* for any changes in beneficiaries, large/expensive items purchased, etc.

E)   Target credit cards and other consumer debt to pay off*; focus on debt used for quickly depreciating items and costliest interest items first.

F)   Diversify*: Check to see that you have your money in enough different types of investments (owned, loaned, liquid, and deferred/special savings), as well as within the types of investments (such as long-term and shorter-term CD's, growth stocks as well as more conservative stocks, etc.)

G)   Update and prioritize your goals using the goal priority list form.

H)   Construct a new spending plan that incorporates all the above for the upcoming year.

I)   Become a regular saver and investor using employer-sponsored savings plans, diversification, compounding and dollar cost averaging.

* Your protection against wealth-robbers

The *QUICK CHECK*
Financial Assessment

This assessment is designed to spot potential holes in your financial security where you might be vulnerable or lacking an important element of your financial base. Unexpected emergencies that occur can find you unprotected and severely disrupt or undermine your family's security or standard of living now or in retirement.

Part I identifies possible areas of need based on general, minimum recommended levels of coverage. These are *general guidelines only*; they are not intended nor held out to be recommendations for action.

Part II provides further clarification and more in-depth reasoning behind the general rule, allowing you to determine if you need to address that area further.

> Every individual's personal financial situation is different, and before you act upon any of these basic guidelines, we recommend you consult a professional with that area of expertise.

The Quick Check
Financial Assessment

Please circle "yes", "no" or "not sure" to each of the following items. When you're through with this section, check off all the items in Part II that you answered "no" or "not sure" to in Part I. Then read through the items you checked off in Part II to see if you need to take further action. If so, record that item on your Action Plan and commit to taking action within 30 days!

ITEM #	DO YOU HAVE:		COVERED?			
1	**EMERGENCY SAVINGS** of at least three to six months' necessary expenses? These funds should be liquid and easily accessible.		NO	YES	NOT SURE	
2	**GROUP (usually employer-provided) SHORT-TERM DISABILITY COVERAGE** for up to six months or one year of disability? You should have coverage that would supply at least 60% of your monthly gross pay.	YOU:	NO	YES	NOT SURE	N/A
		SPOUSE:	NO	YES	NOT SURE	N/A
3	**GROUP (usually employer-provided) LONG-TERM DISABILITY COVERAGE** for disabilities that last until age 65 or life? You should have coverage that would supply at least 60% of your monthly gross pay. Group disability payments are subject to taxation as ordinary income.	YOU:	NO	YES	NOT SURE	N/A
		SPOUSE:	NO	YES	NOT SURE	N/A
4	**PERSONAL DISABILITY COVERAGE** if your employer does not provide sufficient disability coverage? Elimination periods vary. These policies provide approximately 50% to 60% of your gross monthly pay. Personal disability insurance is not subject to income tax.	YOU:	NO	YES	NOT SURE	N/A
		SPOUSE:	NO	YES	NOT SURE	N/A
5	**LIFE INSURANCE COVERAGE** if you have debts or dependents? A <u>general</u> rule of thumb is to have five to seven times the annual value of your services, whether you are employed or are a homemaker.	YOU:	NO	YES	NOT SURE	N/A
		SPOUSE:	NO	YES	NOT SURE	N/A

ITEM #	DO YOU HAVE:		COVERED?			
6	**HEALTH INSURANCE COVERAGE** that covers at least 80% of out-of-hospital expenses, 80% of doctor's charges and 100% of hospitalization and has an overall payment cap of not less than $1,000,000 (i.e., 80/80/100 coverage?)	YOU:	YES	NO	NOT SURE	N/A
		SPOUSE:	YES	NO	NOT SURE	N/A
		CHILDREN:	YES	NO	NOT SURE	N/A
7	**AUTO INSURANCE** that provides at least $100,000 liability coverage, $300,000 total injury coverage and $50,000 coverage for total property damage (i.e., 100/300/50)?	CAR 1:	YES	NO	NOT SURE	N/A
		CAR 2:	YES	NO	NOT SURE	N/A
		CAR 3:	YES	NO	NOT SURE	N/A
8	Have you chosen <u>not</u> to buy **CREDIT INSURANCE** policies on any outstanding loans? Credit insurance is offered by banks, car dealerships, and finance companies to cover your loan payment on a car, boat, home, etc. in the event of your disability or death.	YOU:	YES	NO	NOT SURE	N/A
		SPOUSE:	YES	NO	NOT SURE	N/A
9	**PERSONAL LIABILITY** coverage, also known as an umbrella policy? Standard policy coverage begins at $1 million. If you have an outdoor pool or other potentially dangerous property, teen drivers, a net worth in excess of $100,000 or a high future earnings potential (i.e. a free agent in baseball?), you should have an umbrella policy.	HOME 1:	YES	NO	NOT SURE	N/A
		HOME 2:	YES	NO	NOT SURE	N/A
10	**HOMEOWNER'S OR TENANT'S INSURANCE?** Both of these are available in fairly standard policies known as HO-1 through HO-6, all of which have different coverages available. Special possessions may require additional riders.	HOME 1:	YES	NO	NOT SURE	N/A
		HOME 2:	YES	NO	NOT SURE	N/A
11	**PICTURES,** a written household inventory and/or receipts of home improvements and contents stored somewhere outside your home?	HOME 1:	YES	NO	NOT SURE	N/A
		HOME 2:	YES	NO	NOT SURE	N/A

ITEM #	DO YOU HAVE:		COVERED?			
12	**REPLACEMENT AND INFLATION ENDORSEMENT OPTIONS** on your homeowner's or tenant's insurance? You should have protection that pays you at least 80% of what it takes to replace your loss and an inflation endorsement on your policy.	HOME 1:	YES	NO	NOT SURE	N/A
		HOME 2:	YES	NO	NOT SURE	N/A
13	**UPDATED BENEFICIARIES** of bank, brokerage and retirement accounts and reviewed titles to property ownership within the last three years to reflect any deaths, divorces, marriages or children?	YOU:	YES	NO	NOT SURE	N/A
		SPOUSE:	YES	NO	NOT SURE	N/A
14	A **WILL?** Wills should be updated every three years and revised for changes such as marriage, divorces, births, death, relocation and changes in business situations or tax laws.	YOU:	YES	NO	NOT SURE	N/A
		SPOUSE:	YES	NO	NOT SURE	N/A
15	A **DURABLE POWER OF ATTORNEY?** This lets someone act for you even if you're judged senile or mentally disabled.	YOU:	YES	NO	NOT SURE	N/A
		SPOUSE:	YES	NO	NOT SURE	N/A
16	A **LIVING WILL/PATIENT ADVOCATE?** A living will allows you to appoint someone to exercise your right to refuse treatment that artificially prolongs your dying.	YOU:	YES	NO	NOT SURE	N/A
		SPOUSE:	YES	NO	NOT SURE	N/A
17	A need for **ESTATE PLANNING?** In 2005, if your assets exceed $1.5 million for an individual or $3.0 million for a married couple, your estate will be subject to substantial estate taxes. The estate exclusion amount per person increases to $2.0 million per individual for 2006-2008.	YOU:	YES	NO	NOT SURE	N/A
		SPOUSE:	YES	NO	NOT SURE	N/A

Review of "NO" Responses to the Quick Check Financial Assessment

CHECK IF ANSWERED "NO" OR "NOT SURE"	TOPIC	CHECK IF ACTION IS NEEDED

Check off the left-hand boxes for all items you answered "no" or "not sure" to in Part I. Then read through the items you checked off to see if you need to take further action. If so, record that item on your Action Plan and commit to taking action within 30 days!

1.☐ **EMERGENCY SAVINGS:**

These funds should be liquid and easily accessible. A reserve fund is essentially self-insurance. Minor costs and claims can be expensive to insure; the more savings you have, the less insurance you need. For example, you can increase your car deductibles, eliminate children's life insurance or reduce or eliminate short-term disability policies when you have adequate savings. Three to six months of necessary expenses are highly recommended.

2.☐ **GROUP SHORT-TERM DISABILITY:**

Ninety percent of all disabilities are short-term and last about 13 weeks. If you have an adequate emergency fund or your household does not depend on your income or services, then you do not need this policy. If it is available to you through your employer then take advantage of it since a short-term disability could use up all of your savings. If you need to consider a short-term disability policy but a group plan isn't available to you, review the personal disability policy in item #4.

YOU: _____
SPOUSE: _____

3.☐ **GROUP LONG-TERM DISABILITY:**

Your chances of becoming permanently disabled are <u>five times greater than dying prematurely.</u> A person disabled permanently is a greater financial strain on a family than a person who dies. Again, if your family depends on your income or services and you don't have emergency savings set aside or a personal disability policy, you should ask your benefits department to sign you up. If you don't have group disability available to you, and/or if your family depends on your spouse's income or services and they are not covered by a group plan, review item #4.

YOU: _____
SPOUSE: _____

4.☐   PERSONAL DISABILITY COVERAGE:

If you contribute to the household and you are not covered by a group plan, purchase a personal disability policy. Rarely does a family have the financial resources to handle the economic strain of a long-term disability. The elimination period you choose will depend greatly on the amount of savings you have built up. The longer the elimination period the lower your policy costs will be. Get coverage that is equivalent to 60-65% of your current annual income; make sure the policy is noncancellable and covers you for your "own occupation", meaning that if you become disabled, the insurance company will pay if you can't return to what you were doing before. If you don't get "own occupation" coverage, the insurance company will stop paying if you are mobile enough to empty waste baskets and do light cleaning. Also be sure your coverage is to age 65 or for life.

YOU: _____
SPOUSE: _____

5.☐   LIFE INSURANCE:

If you have debts and/or dependents, buy life insurance. There are two main types of life insurance: term or cash value. Cash value policies such as whole life, universal life, and variable life vary in the way the savings portion feature of the policy is invested and whether you or the insurance company accepts the risk of the value of the investment. Term policies provide "pure" life insurance for people who cannot afford or do not desire the savings feature involved in "cash value" policies. The amount and type you require will depend on your income level, number of dependents, special family needs, outstanding debts and financial goals such as sending all of your children to college, etc. Most Americans are severely under-insured. If you are employed outside of the home, most employers do provide some amount of life insurance automatically; $50,000 is a common amount. This should not be your primary insurance if you have dependents. It can be factored into your personal life insurance needs, however, and help reduce the coverage that you need. If you are single with no dependents and little debt, group life can be sufficient until your lifestyle becomes more complicated. If you are a non-working spouse, you still need enough coverage to pay for the services you provide to your family in the event of your death.

YOU: _____
SPOUSE: _____

6.☐   HEALTH INSURANCE:

If you or any member of your family does not have health insurance, GET IT!!! First, if any member of the family is on an employer-provided plan, see if you can add other family members to it. Next, contact trade or professional organizations you belong to or could join. These often have group health coverage available to members. Lastly, pursue a personal policy. Some health insurers have open enrollment periods where you do not have to pass a health exam to join.

YOU: _____
SPOUSE _____
CHILD: _____

7.☐   AUTO INSURANCE:

An important aspect of auto insurance is liability coverage to protect your wealth in the event that the driver of your car proved to be negligent in an accident. You can be sued for injury, property damage, loss of income and pain and suffering. Liability coverage covers these possibilities as well as legal costs. Consider higher uninsured and underinsured coverage to protect you from those who do not have any insurance at all - the investment is minimal for much greater protection.

_____

8.☐   **CREDIT INSURANCE:**

Credit insurance is very overpriced. It's an additional source of income for the issuer with low cost, like selling you a service warranty on a new refrigerator. Instead of having specific insurance coverage on your loans, you should factor your debts into your need for life insurance.

_____

9.☐   **PERSONAL LIABILITY COVERAGE:**

Umbrella policies for $1,000,000 cost on average around $200 per year. If your assets are under $100,000 and you don't have any unusual risk exposure, then the standard liability on your home should be sufficient coverage. If your net worth exceeds $100,000 or if you have high risk exposure, an umbrella policy can provide important additional coverage.

_____

10.☐   **HOMEOWNER'S OR TENANT'S INSURANCE:**

Most homeowners are required to have insurance and it is incorporated into the mortgage payment. Tenants or apartment dwellers are not required to be insured; only one out of every five renters insures his personal property. Coverage includes not only fire but theft and other perils caused by weather. Tenants policies only cost about $10-$15 per month.

_____

11.☐   **PROOF OF YOUR HOUSEHOLD POSSESSIONS:**

Recent natural disasters are always a poignant reminder of the importance of having a home inventory. At a minimum, videotape your entire home; open drawers, closets, cabinets, etc. Take pictures from a close enough range to show all the contents. Make overall views of your rooms and what's in them. Remember to get the garage, attic, landscaping, tool shed, etc. Talk about each item as you show it, recording the model and price on tape. Your inventory is your guarantee that you'll collect all the protection you paid for. With it, you can make a full list of all your losses. Insurers will generally accept a list you reconstruct from memory. But you'll never recall every item, and those little things add up. When buying insurance most people focus only on their few expensive pieces of furniture. But what drives up the price of refurnishing a home is the pencils and potholders, jackets and mittens, baseballs and houseplants, and other common household items.

_____

12.□ **HOMEOWNER'S INFLATION ENDORSEMENT:**

Newer policies usually have an inflation endorsement policy but older policies might not. Homes should be insured based on replacement value, the standard policy being 80% of fair market value. A portion of your home value is the land which is indestructible and the foundation which is nearly indestructible. Since replacement costs go up every year, instead of upping your policy each year, an inflation endorsement automatically increases your coverage with the rise in construction costs and building code changes. _____

13.□ **BENEFICIARIES AND PROPERTY OWNERSHIP:**

Designated beneficiaries are almost an invisible clause on any bank or brokerage account. Once the original paperwork is done and filed away, you are rarely reminded of who you had listed on your accounts. Death, divorce, marriage and additional children will normally cause beneficiaries to be changed, but this process is often overlooked and the intended party suffers. Also, property owned jointly skips probate (a time-consuming legal process), while individually-owned property in an estate must go through probate.

YOU: _____
SPOUSE: _____

14.□ **WILLS:**

If you die without a will, your estate will be divided up by the state according to the state laws of intestacy. If you are single, this usually means the state will distribute your assets first to your surviving parents, then equally to your siblings. If you are married, this means (in most states) that your spouse will receive one third to one half of your estate and any children would equally split the rest. It also means the state would choose guardians for your children if both of you should unexpectedly die. Lastly, the state chooses an administrator for your estate settlement when no will exists. Wills allow your wishes to be executed and your surviving dependents/family/friends to be cared for in the way you see fit. It is also recommended that you draft a "letter of instruction" that details where important documents are located and what you would like done about your burial.

YOU: _____
SPOUSE: _____

15.□ **DURABLE POWER OF ATTORNEY:**

Everyone needs a backup - a person to act for you if you're away, if you're sick, if you get hit by a car and can't function for a while, or if you grow senile. That means giving someone - a spouse, a parent, an adult child, a trusted friend - your power of attorney. A durable power of attorney lasts, while other powers don't. As long as you are mentally capable, you can revoke a durable power whenever you like. You have to execute a new durable power every four or five years, to show that your intention holds. Insurance companies and financial institutions probably won't honor an old power.
If you'd rather not trust anyone until you absolutely have to, write a springing power of attorney. It doesn't take effect unless you become mentally incapacitated, and the document defines exactly what that means.

YOU: _____
SPOUSE: _____

16.☐   **LIVING WILL/PATIENT ADVOCATE:**

Anyone who has seen a dying or comatose parent hooked up to life-support machines
understands the issue of the right to die. Decision making for the family is difficult under
times of great emotional stress. The situation can become one that also impacts family
finances. The medical action that is or is not taken under those circumstances can be one
dictated by the patient, <u>provided</u> the situation has been fully considered while of sound mind
and body. Please make clear your views to your immediate family and physicians. Most
states have available "Living Wills" and/or durable powers of attorney for health care.
Contact your local bar association for more information.

                                                                              YOU: _____
                                                                              SPOUSE: _____

17.☐   **ESTATE PLANNING:**

For 2005, for an individual with assets exceeding $1.5 million after debts have been
satisfied, or a married couple with assets exceeding $3.0 million after their debts have been
satisfied, an estate planner can help you employ the tax savings strategies most suitable for
your situation. Strategies include giving your assets away while you are alive to intended
beneficiaries, creating trusts to generate income for your needs and gifting assets to
charitable institutions. Gifting and utilizing trusts require careful and professional planning.
The level of assets excluded from federal estate taxation increases in 2006-2008 to reach a
level of $2.0 million per person and eventually $3.5 million per person in 2009.

                                                                              YOU: _____
                                                                              SPOUSE: _____

Charting Your Level of Debt

Fill in the amounts that you owe to various sources for tracking the change in your level of debt.

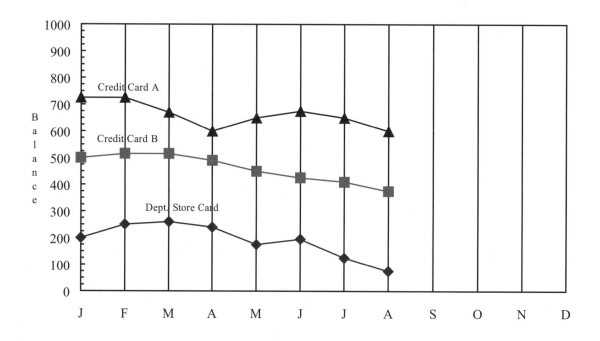

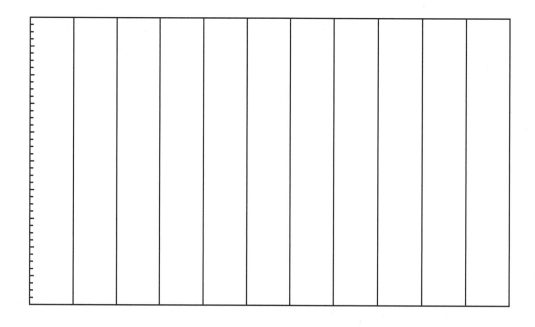

Tracking Your Level of Debt

Fill in the amounts that you owe to various sources for tracking the change in your level of debt.

List your debt sources in order of highest interest charging source first, or in order of smallest balances first. Include your mortgage (if you have one) to provide a broader perspective.

Name of Lender	*Interest Charged*	*Estimated Balance*	*Minimum Monthly Payment*	*Targeted Monthly Payment*
_____	_____ %	_____	_____	_____
_____	_____ %	_____	_____	_____
_____	_____ %	_____	_____	_____
_____	_____ %	_____	_____	_____
_____	_____ %	_____	_____	_____
_____	_____ %	_____	_____	_____
_____	_____ %	_____	_____	_____
_____	_____ %	_____	_____	_____
Totals		$ _____	$ _____	$ _____

Tracking Your Net Worth

Fill in the dollar amounts and the years below for tracking the growth of your net worth.

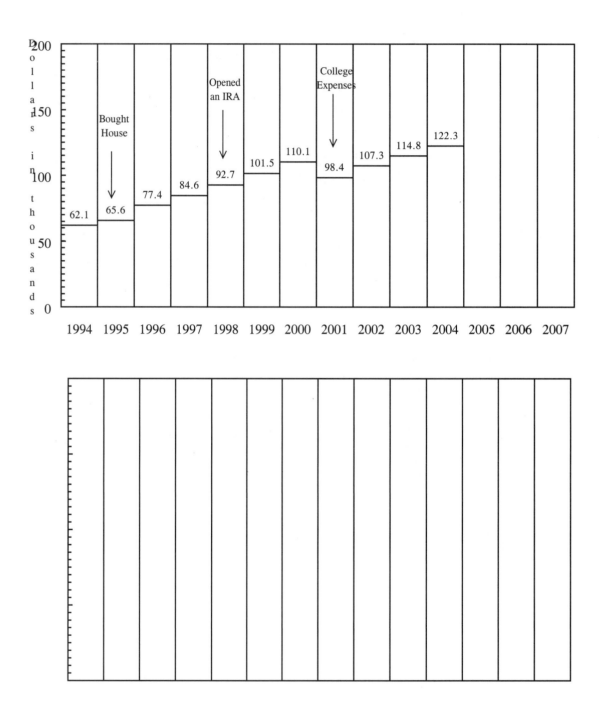

Net Worth Summary

Finish transferring the values of each section listed below from the prior worksheets. See the example in the appendix for more information.

	Estimated Current Value	As a % of Total Assets	Estimated Average Return Earned
I) What You Own (Assets):			
A) Total Liquid Assets ....(from page 23)	$ _____	_____%	1-4%
B) Total Loaned Assets ....(from page 24)	_____	_____	3-7%
C) Total Owned Assets ....(from page 25)	_____	_____	6-12%
D) Total Personal Assets ....(from page 26)	_____	_____	-20% or more per year
E) Total Deferred & Special Assets .(from page 27)	_____	_____	6-12%
Total Assets, or What You Own	$ _____	100 %	

	Estimated Balance	As a % of Total Debts	Average Interest Rate Paid
II) What You Owe (Liabilities):			
F) Total Short-Term Debt ....(from page 28)	$ _____	_____%	12-23%
G) Total Intermediate-Term Debt ..(from page 28)	_____	_____	6-12%
H) Total Long-Term Debt ....(from page 28)	_____	_____	5-9%
Total Liabilities, or What You Owe	$ _____	100 %	

YOUR NET WORTH = $ _____

    OWN (I) – OWE (II)

List of Potential Goals

1) Circle all those goals that are important to you
2) Place a checkmark for each goal as to whether it is essential, important, or nice
3) Rate the goals within each category (essential, important, nice) by numbering them 1–5, with 1 being most important.

Goal	Essential		Important		Nice	
New house or bigger house						
Second house (vacation home, time share unit, etc.)						
Interior home improvement (furniture, appliances, redecorating)						
Exterior home improvement (landscaping, roofing, additions, etc.)						
New car or second car						
Recreational vehicles (mobile homes, boat, snowmobiles, etc.)						
Home electronics (stereo, VCR, computer, etc.)						
New clothing						
Enrichment programs for children (ballet, music, sports, etc.)						
Vacation or major travel/adventure programs						
Gifts for grandchildren, spouse, family, etc.						
Emergency savings						
Debt reduction						
Personal (taxable) investment program						
401(k) or other retirement fund						
College fund for children						
Continuing education (college enrichment)						
Will and estate plan drawn up						
Start/expand a business						
Career change (anticipated income reduction or expansion)						
Quality of life (sacrificing additional income to be with family)						
New hobby (crafts, sports, building things, etc.)						
Increase charitable contributions						
Volunteering more time to church, non-profit organizations, etc.						
Other						
Other						

Identifying
Needs vs. Wants

Most of us don't have the money or the time to tackle all of our potential goals at the same time. The point of this exercise is to bring more focus to the list you created on the prior page by identifying which goals are needs and which are wants.

The way to successfully accomplish your goals is to match your potential goals to the values you identified earlier. This way, the goals are more meaningful and you will be more motivated to make them happen.

Record your top three values from page 36 in the left hand column. Then try to match your essential and important goals to one or more of your top personal values. Finish by evaluating your list and assigning a goal number of 1-6. Those that didn't make the top six for now will have to wait until you've completed one or more of the items on this list first.

Top Personal Values	*Description of Goal*	*Goal Number*
1) _____	• _____	_____
	• _____	_____
	• _____	_____
	• _____	_____
2) _____	• _____	_____
	• _____	_____
	• _____	_____
	• _____	_____
3) _____	• _____	_____
	• _____	_____
	• _____	_____
	• _____	_____

In order for goals to be accomplished, they need to be SMART:

S pecific
M easurable
A ttainable
R ealistic
T arget date to accomplish

The following worksheet will help you be SMART with your money. To complete, follow the instructions on the prior page.

	(1) Priority Goals	(2) Total Amount Needed	(3) Time Frame (number of months)	(4) Amt. Needed/ Month (Column 2 / Column 3)	(5) Amount Already Allocated	(6) Amount Needed Per Month (Column 4 - Column 5)
Goal #6:						
Goal #5:						
Goal #4:						
Goal #3:						
Goal #2:						
Goal #1:						
Example: Goal #1: Pay off credit cards		$5,000	12	$420	$250	$170/mo.
Totals		$		$	$	$

Twelve Month Spending Plan

As of: _____

SOURCES OF INCOME	PROJECTED (AVERAGE)	1	2	3	4	5	6	7	8	9	10	11	12	12 MONTH TOTAL
Partner A (after-tax)														
Partner B (after-tax)														
Bonuses/Commission														
Interest/Dividends														
Rents/Royalties														
Other _____														
Other _____														
Other _____														
A. TOTAL INCOME BY MONTH														
Subtract Anticipated Monthly Expenses														
CASH AVAILABLE/ CASH NEEDED ±														

Planned Expenditures For the Month			
B. Actual Expenditures For the Month			
Amount Under ( ) or Over + (A – B)			

CATEGORY	*	PROJ AVG	#	1	2	3	4	5	6	7	8	9	10	11	12	12 MONTH TOTAL
FIXED COSTS:																
Goal																
Goal																
Goal																
PERIODIC COSTS:																
TOTAL FIXED & PERIODIC COSTS																

CATEGORY	*	PROJ AVG	#	1	2	3	4	5	6	7	8	9	10	11	12	12 MO. TOTAL
VARIABLE COSTS:																
Goal																
Goal																
Goal																
TOTAL VARIABLE COSTS																

DEBT TRACKING	#	1	2	3	4	5	6	7	8	9	10	11	12	BAL.

Variable Spending Tracking Sheet

For the month: _____

Instructions for tracking your variable spending:

1) Set up spending item categories in the far left "Item" column in the same order as shown on your spending plan form.

2) Every evening, record (in pencil) the cash you spent that day (cash only; checks written will be done later).

3) At the end of every month, review your check book and fill in what you spent on various days in the various spending categories.

4) Then, total the rows for each spending category and compare to what was budgeted; make adjustments on your spending plan for the future as needed.

ITEM	1	2	3	4	5	6	7	8	9	10	11	12	13	14	15	16	17	18	19	20	21	22	23	24	25	26	27	28	29	30	31	TOTALS
Gas																																
Snacks																																
Coffee																																
Magazine																																
Newspprs																																
Cigarette																																
Car Wash																																
Eat Out																																
Movies																																

Appendix B:
Sample Financial Plan

Appendix B: Sample Financial Plan

At the end of each section of this book, we will stop and direct you to record your Action Ideas on this Action Plan. When you have completed the workbook, tear this page out and post it on your refrigerator, your bathroom mirror, or keep it with your monthly bills as a reminder to complete the actions you have determined during the program.

My Action Plan

First Base

Determine Where You Are

Quick Check Financial Assessment (page 11)

<u>*Actions I Need To Take*</u>	<u>*Target Date*</u>
1) *Increase emergency savings*	*Immediately*
2) *Personal disability coverage*	*February*
3) *Pictures of house/inventory*	*Immediately*
4) *Add replacement cost to homeowners*	*March*
4) *Update beneficiaries*	*March*

Net Worth Actions to Take (page 29)

My Net Worth Isn't As Strong As It Could Be Because:	*Ways to Strengthen My Net Worth:*
Too much debt	*Pay off debt*
Not enough emergency cash	*Set-up monthly savings*
Interest rates too high	*Refinance debt*

With my next raise I will: *Pay off debt*

With my next windfall I will: *Increase retirement savings*

Determine Where You Want to Go

Second Base

Values-Based Goal Setting:

In the next one to three years, it is very important to me that I accomplish the following goals (page 41):

Goal	Total Amount Needed	Amount Needed Per Month
1) *Pay off debt*	*$3,000*	*$250*
2) *Build emergency savings*	*$6,000*	*$333*
2) *Increase retirement saving*	*?*	*$200*

How to Confidently Accomplish Your Goals

Third Base

Wealth-building techniques that I will use to help me meet my goals (pages 45 to 64):

	Technique	Application	Goal
Example:	Debt Reduction	Consolidate Debt	Eliminate Credit Card Debt
1)	*Diversification*	*In retirement Savings*	*Decrease risk*
2)	*Compounding*	*Retirement*	*Have more money*
3)	*Dollar Cost Averaging*	*Investing*	*Retirement*

Implement Your Plan

Home

From the spending plan worksheets on pages 75 to 79:

I can find $ *300* per month to apply towards my goals.

I will begin using my spending plan as of *February* (month).

The *QUICK CHECK* Financial Assessment

This assessment is designed to spot potential holes in your financial security where you might be vulnerable or lacking an important element of your financial base. Unexpected emergencies that occur can find you unprotected and severely disrupt or undermine your family's security or standard of living now or in retirement.

Part I   identifies possible areas of need based on general, minimum recommended levels of coverage. These are *general guidelines only*; they are not intended nor held out to be recommendations for action.

Part II   provides further clarification and more in-depth reasoning behind the general rule, allowing you to determine if you need to address that area further.

> Every individual's personal financial situation is different, and before you act upon any of these basic guidelines, we recommend you consult a professional with that area of expertise.

The *Quick Check* Financial Assessment

Please circle "yes', "no" or "not sure" to each of the following items. When you're through with this section, check off all the items in Part II that you answered "no" or "not sure" to in Part I. Then read through the items you checked off in Part II to see if you need to take further action. If so, record that item on your Action Plan and commit to taking action within 30 days!

ITEM #	DO YOU HAVE:		COVERED?			
1	**EMERGENCY SAVINGS** of at least three to six months' necessary expenses? These funds should be liquid and easily accessible.		(NO)	YES	NOT SURE	
2	**GROUP (usually employer-provided) SHORT-TERM DISABILITY COVERAGE** for up to six months or one year of disability? You should have coverage that would supply at least 60% of your monthly gross pay.	YOU:	NO	(YES)	NOT SURE	N/A
		SPOUSE:	NO	(YES)	NOT SURE	N/A
3	**GROUP (usually employer-provided) LONG-TERM DISABILITY COVERAGE** for disabilities that last until age 65 or life? You should have coverage that would supply at least 60% of your monthly gross pay. Group disability payments are subject to taxation as ordinary income.	YOU:	NO	(YES)	NOT SURE	N/A
		SPOUSE:	NO	(YES)	NOT SURE	N/A
4	**PERSONAL DISABILITY COVERAGE** if your employer does not provide sufficient disability coverage? Elimination periods vary. These policies provide approximately 50% to 60% of your gross monthly pay. Personal disability insurance is not subject to income tax.	YOU:	(NO)	YES	NOT SURE	N/A
		SPOUSE:	(NO)	YES	NOT SURE	N/A
5	**LIFE INSURANCE COVERAGE** if you have debts or dependents? A <u>general</u> rule of thumb is to have five to seven times the annual value of your services, whether you are employed or are a homemaker.	YOU:	NO	(YES)	NOT SURE	N/A
		SPOUSE:	NO	(YES)	NOT SURE	N/A

113

DISCOVER LEARNING®

Appendix B: Sample Financial Plan

ITEM #	DO YOU HAVE:		COVERED?			
6	**HEALTH INSURANCE COVERAGE** that covers at least 80% of out-of-hospital expenses, 80% of doctor's charges and 100% of hospitalization and has an overall payment cap of not less than $1,000,000 (i.e., 80/80/100 coverage?)	YOU:	(YES)	NO	NOT SURE	N/A
		SPOUSE:	(YES)	NO	NOT SURE	N/A
		CHILDREN:	(YES)	NO	NOT SURE	N/A
7	**AUTO INSURANCE** that provides at least $100,000 liability coverage, $300,000 total injury coverage and $50,000 coverage for total property damage (i.e., 100/300/50)?	CAR 1:	(YES)	NO	NOT SURE	N/A
		CAR 2:	(YES)	NO	NOT SURE	N/A
		CAR 3:	(YES)	NO	NOT SURE	N/A
8	Have you chosen <u>not</u> to buy **CREDIT INSURANCE** policies on any outstanding loans? Credit insurance is offered by banks, car dealerships, and finance companies to cover your loan payment on a car, boat, home, etc. in the event of your disability or death.	YOU:	YES	NO	(NOT SURE)	N/A
		SPOUSE:	YES	NO	(NOT SURE)	N/A
9	**PERSONAL LIABILITY** coverage, also known as an umbrella policy? Standard policy coverage begins at $1 million. If you have an outdoor pool or other potentially dangerous property, teen drivers, a net worth in excess of $100,000 or a high future earnings potential (i.e. a free agent in baseball?), you should have an umbrella policy.	HOME 1:	YES	NO	(NOT SURE)	N/A
		HOME 2:	YES	NO	(NOT SURE)	N/A
10	**HOMEOWNER'S OR TENANT'S INSURANCE?** Both of these are available in fairly standard policies known as HO-1 through HO-6, all of which have different coverages available. Special possessions may require additional riders.	HOME 1:	(YES)	NO	NOT SURE	N/A
		HOME 2:	(YES)	NO	NOT SURE	N/A
11	**PICTURES,** a written household inventory and/or receipts of home improvements and contents stored somewhere outside your home?	HOME 1:	YES	(NO)	NOT SURE	N/A
		HOME 2:	YES	NO	NOT SURE	(N/A)

114

ITEM #	DO YOU HAVE:		COVERED?				
12	**REPLACEMENT AND INFLATION ENDORSEMENT OPTIONS** on your homeowner's or tenant's insurance? You should have protection that pays you at least 80% of what it takes to replace your loss and an inflation endorsement on your policy.	HOME 1:	YES	NO	(NOT SURE)	N/A	
		HOME 2:	YES	NO	NOT SURE	(N/A)	
13	**UPDATED BENEFICIARIES** of bank, brokerage and retirement accounts and reviewed titles to property ownership within the last three years to reflect any deaths, divorces, marriages or children?	YOU:	YES	(NO)	NOT SURE	N/A	
		SPOUSE:	YES	(NO)	NOT SURE	N/A	
14	A **WILL?** Wills should be updated every three years and revised for changes such as marriage, divorces, births, death, relocation and changes in business situations or tax laws.	YOU:	YES	(NO)	NOT SURE	N/A	
		SPOUSE:	YES	(NO)	NOT SURE	N/A	
15	A **DURABLE POWER OF ATTORNEY?** This lets someone act for you even if you're judged senile or mentally disabled.	YOU:	YES	(NO)	NOT SURE	N/A	
		SPOUSE:	YES	(NO)	NOT SURE	N/A	
16	A **LIVING WILL/PATIENT ADVOCATE?** A living will allows you to appoint someone to exercise your right to refuse treatment that artificially prolongs your dying.	YOU:	YES	(NO)	NOT SURE	N/A	
		SPOUSE:	YES	(NO)	NOT SURE	N/A	
17	A need for **ESTATE PLANNING?** In 2005, if your assets exceed $1.5 million for an individual or $3.0 million for a married couple, your estate will be subject to substantial estate taxes. The estate exclusion amount per person increases to $2.0 million per individual for 2006-2008.	YOU:	YES	NO	(NOT SURE)	N/A	
		SPOUSE:	YES	NO	(NOT SURE)	N/A	

Appendix B: Sample Financial Plan

Review of "NO" Responses to the Quick Check Financial Assessment

CHECK IF ANSWERED "NO" OR "NOT SURE"	TOPIC	CHECK IF ACTION IS NEEDED

Check off the left-hand boxes for all items you answered "no" or "not sure" to in Part I. Then read through the items you checked off to see if you need to take further action. If so, record that item on your Action Plan and commit to taking action within 30 days!

1. ☑ **EMERGENCY SAVINGS:**

    These funds should be liquid and easily accessible. A reserve fund is essentially self-insurance. Minor costs and claims can be expensive to insure; the more savings you have, the less insurance you need. For example, you can increase your car deductibles, eliminate children's life insurance or reduce or eliminate short-term disability policies when you have adequate savings. Three to six months of necessary expenses are highly recommended. ✓

2. ☐ **GROUP SHORT-TERM DISABILITY:**

    Ninety percent of all disabilities are short-term and last about 13 weeks. If you have an adequate emergency fund or your household does not depend on your income or services, then you do not need this policy. If it is available to you through your employer then take advantage of it since a short-term disability could use up all of your savings. If you need to consider a short-term disability policy but a group plan isn't available to you, review the personal disability policy in item #4. **YOU:** _____ **SPOUSE:** _____

3. ☐ **GROUP LONG-TERM DISABILITY:**

    Your chances of becoming permanently disabled are <u>five times greater than dying prematurely.</u> A person disabled permanently is a greater financial strain on a family than a person who dies. Again, if your family depends on your income or services and you don't have emergency savings set aside or a personal disability policy, you should ask your benefits department to sign you up. If you don't have group disability available to you, and/or if your family depends on your spouse's income or services and they are not covered by a group plan, review item #4. **YOU:** _____ **SPOUSE:** _____

4. ☑ **PERSONAL DISABILITY COVERAGE:**

If you contribute to the household and you are not covered by a group plan, purchase a personal disability policy. Rarely does a family have the financial resources to handle the economic strain of a long-term disability. The elimination period you choose will depend greatly on the amount of savings you have built up. The longer the elimination period the lower your policy costs will be. Get coverage that is equivalent to 60-65% of your current annual income; make sure the policy is noncancellable and covers you for your "own occupation", meaning that if you become disabled, the insurance company will pay if you can't return to what you were doing before. If you don't get "own occupation" coverage, the insurance company will stop paying if you are mobile enough to empty waste baskets and do light cleaning. Also be sure your coverage is to age 65 or for life.

YOU: ✓
SPOUSE: ✓

5. ☑ **LIFE INSURANCE:**

If you have debts and/or dependents, buy life insurance. There are two main types of life insurance: term or cash value. Cash value policies such as whole life, universal life, and variable life vary in the way the savings portion feature of the policy is invested and whether you or the insurance company accepts the risk of the value of the investment. Term policies provide "pure" life insurance for people who cannot afford or do not desire the savings feature involved in "cash value" policies. The amount and type you require will depend on your income level, number of dependents, special family needs, outstanding debts and financial goals such as sending all of your children to college, etc. Most Americans are severely under-insured. If you are employed outside of the home, most employers do provide some amount of life insurance automatically; $50,000 is a common amount. This should not be your primary insurance if you have dependents. It can be factored into your personal life insurance needs, however, and help reduce the coverage that you need. If you are single with no dependents and little debt, group life can be sufficient until your lifestyle becomes more complicated. If you are a non-working spouse, you still need enough coverage to pay for the services you provide to your family in the event of your death.

YOU: no
SPOUSE: ✓

6. ☐ **HEALTH INSURANCE:**

If you or any member of your family does not have health insurance, GET IT!!! First, if any member of the family is on an employer-provided plan, see if you can add other family members to it. Next, contact trade or professional organizations you belong to or could join. These often have group health coverage available to members. Lastly, pursue a personal policy. Some health insurers have open enrollment periods where you do not have to pass a health exam to join.

YOU: _____
SPOUSE _____
CHILD: _____

7. ☐ **AUTO INSURANCE:**

An important aspect of auto insurance is liability coverage to protect your wealth in the event that the driver of your car proved to be negligent in an accident. You can be sued for injury, property damage, loss of income and pain and suffering. Liability coverage covers these possibilities as well as legal costs. Consider higher uninsured and underinsured coverage to protect you from those who do not have any insurance at all - the investment is minimal for much greater protection.

_____

8.☑ CREDIT INSURANCE:

Credit insurance is very overpriced. It's an additional source of income for the issuer with low cost, like selling you a service warranty on a new refrigerator. Instead of having specific insurance coverage on your loans, you should factor your debts into your need for life insurance.

Check
on

9.☑ PERSONAL LIABILITY COVERAGE:

Umbrella policies for $1,000,000 cost on average around $200 per year. If your assets are under $100,000 and you don't have any unusual risk exposure, then the standard liability on your home should be sufficient coverage. If your net worth exceeds $100,000 or if you have high risk exposure, an umbrella policy can provide important additional coverage.

✓

10.☐ HOMEOWNER'S OR TENANT'S INSURANCE:

Most homeowners are required to have insurance and it is incorporated into the mortgage payment. Tenants or apartment dwellers are not required to be insured; only one out of every five renters insures his personal property. Coverage includes not only fire but theft and other perils caused by weather. Tenants policies only cost about $10-$15 per month.

11.☑ PROOF OF YOUR HOUSEHOLD POSSESSIONS:

Recent natural disasters are always a poignant reminder of the importance of having a home inventory. At a minimum, videotape your entire home; open drawers, closets, cabinets, etc. Take pictures from a close enough range to show all the contents. Make overall views of your rooms and what's in them. Remember to get the garage, attic, landscaping, tool shed, etc. Talk about each item as you show it, recording the model and price on tape. Your inventory is your guarantee that you'll collect all the protection you paid for. With it, you can make a full list of all your losses. Insurers will generally accept a list you reconstruct from memory. But you'll never recall every item, and those little things add up. When buying insurance most people focus only on their few expensive pieces of furniture. But what drives up the price of refurnishing a home is the pencils and potholders, jackets and mittens, baseballs and houseplants, and other common household items.

✓

12.☑ **HOMEOWNER'S INFLATION ENDORSEMENT:**

Newer policies usually have an inflation endorsement policy but older policies might not. Homes should be insured based on replacement value, the standard policy being 80% of fair market value. A portion of your home value is the land which is indestructible and the foundation which is nearly indestructible. Since replacement costs go up every year, instead of upping your policy each year, an inflation endorsement automatically increases your coverage with the rise in construction costs and building code changes.

✓

13.☑ **BENEFICIARIES AND PROPERTY OWNERSHIP:**

Designated beneficiaries are almost an invisible clause on any bank or brokerage account. Once the original paperwork is done and filed away, you are rarely reminded of who you had listed on your accounts. Death, divorce, marriage and additional children will normally cause beneficiaries to be changed, but this process is often overlooked and the intended party suffers. Also, property owned jointly skips probate (a time-consuming legal process), while individually-owned property in an estate must go through probate.

YOU: ✓
SPOUSE: ✓

14.☑ **WILLS:**

If you die without a will, your estate will be divided up by the state according to the state laws of intestacy. If you are single, this usually means the state will distribute your assets first to your surviving parents, then equally to your siblings. If you are married, this means (in most states) that your spouse will receive one third to one half of your estate and any children would equally split the rest. It also means the state would choose guardians for your children if both of you should unexpectedly die. Lastly, the state chooses an administrator for your estate settlement when no will exists. Wills allow your wishes to be executed and your surviving dependents/family/friends to be cared for in the way you see fit. It is also recommended that you draft a "letter of instruction" that details where important documents are located and what you would like done about your burial.

YOU: ✓
SPOUSE: ✓

15.☑ **DURABLE POWER OF ATTORNEY:**

Everyone needs a backup - a person to act for you if you're away, if you're sick, if you get hit by a car and can't function for a while, or if you grow senile. That means giving someone - a spouse, a parent, an adult child, a trusted friend - your power of attorney. A durable power of attorney lasts, while other powers don't. As long as you are mentally capable, you can revoke a durable power whenever you like. You have to execute a new durable power every four or five years, to show that your intention holds. Insurance companies and financial institutions probably won't honor an old power.
If you'd rather not trust anyone until you absolutely have to, write a springing power of attorney. It doesn't take effect unless you become mentally incapacitated, and the document defines exactly what that means.

YOU: ✓
SPOUSE: ✓

Appendix B: Sample Financial Plan

16.☑ **LIVING WILL/PATIENT ADVOCATE:**

Anyone who has seen a dying or comatose parent hooked up to life-support machines understands the issue of the right to die. Decision making for the family is difficult under times of great emotional stress. The situation can become one that also impacts family finances. The medical action that is or is not taken under those circumstances can be one dictated by the patient, <u>provided</u> the situation has been fully considered while of sound mind and body. Please make clear your views to your immediate family and physicians. Most states have available "Living Wills" and/or durable powers of attorney for health care. Contact your local bar association for more information.

YOU: ✓
SPOUSE: ✓

17.☑ **ESTATE PLANNING:**

For 2005, an individual with assets exceeding $1.5 million after debts have been satisfied, or a married couple with assets exceeding $3.0 million after their debts have been satisfied, an estate planner can help you employ the tax savings strategies most suitable for your situation. Strategies include giving your assets away while you are alive to intended beneficiaries, creating trusts to generate income for your needs and gifting assets to charitable institutions. Gifting and utilizing trusts require careful and professional planning. The level of assets excluded from federal estate taxation increases in 2006-2008 to reach a level of $2.0 million per person and eventually $3.5 million per person in 2009.

YOU: _____
SPOUSE: _____

Net Worth Summary

Age: 45

Finish transferring the values of each section listed below from the prior worksheets. See the example in the appendix for more information.

I) What You Own (Assets):

	Estimated Current Value	As a % of Total Assets	Estimated Average Return Earned
A) Total Liquid Assets . . . .(from page 23)	$ 4,500	2 %	1-4%
B) Total Loaned Assets . . . . (from page 24)	10,500	4	3-7%
C) Total Owned Assets . . . .(from page 25)	150,000	65	6-12%
D) Total Personal Assets . . . . (from page 26)	21,000	9	-20% or more per year
E) Total Deferred & Special Assets .(from page 27)	45,000	20	6-12%
Total Assets, or What You Own	$ 231,000	**100 %**	

II) What You Owe (Liabilities):

	Estimated Balance	As a % of Total Debts	Average Interest Rate Paid
F) Total Short-Term Debt . . . .(from page 28)	$ 3,000	3	12-23%
G) Total Intermediate-Term Debt . .(from page 28)	15,000	13	6-12%
H) Total Long-Term Debt . . . .(from page 28)	101,000	84	5-9%
Total Liabilities, or What You Owe	$ 119,000	**100 %**	

YOUR NET WORTH =
OWN (I)– OWE (II)

$ 112,000

Tracking Your Level of Debt

Fill in the amounts that you owe to various sources for tracking the change in your level of debt.

List your debt sources in order of highest interest charging source first, or in order of smallest balances first. Include your mortgage (if you have one) to provide a broader perspective.

Name of Lender	Interest Charged	Estimated Balance	Minimum Monthly Payment	Targeted Monthly Payment
Sears	22 %	500	100	100
JC Penney	21 %	1,000	150	250
Visa	14 %	1,500	100	250
Car loan	9 %	7,000	275	275
Student loan	8 %	8,000	50	50
Mortgage	7 %	101,000	850	850
	%			
	%			
Totals		$119,000	$ 1,525	$ 1,775

List of Potential Goals

1) Circle all those goals that are important to you
2) Place a checkmark for each goal as to whether it is essential, important, or nice
3) Rate the goals within each category (essential, important, nice) by numbering them 1–5, with 1 being most important.

Goal	Essential		Important		Nice	
New house or bigger house					6	
Second house (vacation home, time share unit, etc.)						
Interior home improvement (furniture, appliances, redecorating)						
Exterior home improvement (landscaping, roofing, additions, etc.)						
New car or second car			5			
Recreational vehicles (mobile homes, boat, snowmobiles, etc.)						
Home electronics (stereo, VCR, computer, etc.)						
New clothing						
Enrichment programs for children (ballet, music, sports, etc.)						
Vacation or major travel/adventure programs						
Gifts for grandchildren, spouse, family, etc.						
Emergency savings	2					
Debt reduction	1					
Personal (taxable) investment program						
401(k) or other retirement fund	3					
College fund for children						
Continuing education (college enrichment)						
Will and estate plan drawn up	4					
Start/expand a business						
Career change (anticipated income reduction or expansion)						
Quality of life (sacrificing additional income to be with family)						
New hobby (crafts, sports, building things, etc.)						
Increase charitable contributions						
Volunteering more time to church, non-profit organizations, etc.						
Other						
Other						

Identifying
Needs vs. Wants

Most of us don't have the money or the time to tackle all of our potential goals at the same time. The point of this exercise is to bring more focus to the list you created on the prior page by identifying which goals are needs and which are wants.

The way to successfully accomplish your goals is to match your potential goals to the values you identified earlier. This way, the goals are more meaningful and you will be more motivated to make them happen.

Record your top three values from page 36 in the left hand column. Then try to match your essential and important goals to one or more of your top personal values. Finish by evaluating your list and assigning a goal number of 1-6. Those that didn't make the top six for now will have to wait until you've completed one or more of the items on this list first.

Top Personal Values	Description of Goal	Goal Number
1) *True to God*	• Pay off debt	1
	• Emergency savings	2
	• Will and estate plan	4
	• _____	___
	• _____	___
2) *True to self*	• Pay off debt	1
	• Emergency savings	2
	• 401(k) fund	3
	• New car	6
	• New house	5
3) *Good spouse and parent*	• Pay off debt	1
	• Emergency savings	2
	• 401(k) fund	3
	• Will and estate plan	4
	• New house	6

In order for goals to be accomplished, they need to be SMART:

S pecific
M easurable
A ttainable
R ealistic
T arget date to accomplish

The following worksheet will help you be SMART with your money. To complete, follow the instructions on the prior page.

(1) Priority Goals	(2) Total Amount Needed	(3) Time Frame (number of months)	(4) Amt. Needed/ Month (Column 2 / Column 3)	(5) Amount Already Allocated	(6) Amount Needed Per Month (Column 4 - Column 5)
Goal #6: New house	?				?
Goal #5: New car	?	48	$350	$275	$75
Goal #4: Will and estate plan	$1000	12	$83	$0	$83
Goal #3: Increase 401(k) savings	?	ongoing	$500	$300	$200
Goal #2: Build emergency savings	$6000	18	$333	$0	$333
Goal #1: Pay off debt	$3000	5	$600	$350	$250
Totals			$1,866	$925	$941

Twelve Month Spending Plan

As of: _____

SOURCES OF INCOME	PROJECTED (AVERAGE)	1 M	2 A	3 M	4 J	5 J	6 A	7 S	8 O	9	10	11	12	12 MONTH TOTAL
Partner A (after-tax)	3,300	3300	3800	3300	3300									
Partner B (after-tax)	1,500	1500	1500	1500	1700									
Bonuses/Commission														
Interest/Dividends														
Rents/Royalties														
Other _____														
Other _____														
Other _____														
A. TOTAL INCOME BY MONTH	4,800	4800	5300	4800	5000									
Subtract Anticipated Monthly Expenses	4,775	4800	5400	4600	4900									
CASH AVAILABLE/ CASH NEEDED $\pm$	+25	0	(100)	+200	+100									

		1	2	3	4	5	6	7	8	9	10	11	12	
Planned Expenditures For the Month		4800	5400	4600	4900									
B. Actual Expenditures For the Month		4800	5500	4750	4850									
Amount Under ( ) or Over + (A − B)		0	(200)	+50	+150									

126

CATEGORY	*	PROJ AVG	#	1 M	2 A	3 M	4 J	5 J	6 A	7 S	8 O	9	10	11	12	12 MONTH TOTAL
FIXED COSTS:																
Mortgage		50														
Heat		50														
Electric		75														
Phone		75														
Car Ins		50														
Life Ins		50														
Cable		30														
Car Payment		275														
Goal Debt Reduction		600	1	600	600	600	600	600	–	–	–					
Goal Emerg. Savings	*	0	2	–	–	–	–	–	333	333	333					
Goal 401(k)		300	3	–	–	–	–	–	200	200	200					
PERIODIC COSTS:																
Christmas	*															
Taxes									1000							
Water Bill				50			100			100						
TOTAL FIXED & PERIODIC COSTS		1555														

CATEGORY	*	PROJ AVG	#	1 M	2 A	3 M	4 J	5 J	6 A	7 S	8 O	9	10	11	12	12 MO. TOTAL
VARIABLE COSTS:																
Mad Money		250		250	250	250	250	250	250	250	250					
Food		600		600	600	600	600	600	600	600	600					
Auto Gas		80		80	80	80	80	80	80	80	80					
Eating Out		60		60	60	60	60	60	60	60	60					
Donations		400		400	400	400	400	400	400	400	400					
Misc.		100		100	100	100	100	100	100	100	100					
Clothing		100		100	100	100	100	100	100	100	100					
Entertainment		100		100	100	100	100	100	100	100	100					
Haircuts		30		30	30	30	30	30	30	30	30					
Child Care		450		450	450	450	450	450	450	450	450					
Vacations		150		150	150	150	150	150	150	150	150					
Gifts		50		50	50	50	50	50	50	50	50					
Music Lessons		50		50	50	50	50	50	50	50	50					
TOTAL VARIABLE COSTS		2420		2420	2420	2420	2420	2420	2420	2420	2420					

DEBT TRACKING	#	1	2	3	4	5	6	7	8	9	10	11	12	BAL.
Sears	1	100	100	100	100	100	–	–	–					
JC Penney	1	250	250	250	250	250	–	–	–					
Visa	1	250	250	250	250	250	–	–	–					

128

Variable Spending Tracking Sheet

For the month: _____

Instructions for tracking your variable spending:

1) Set up spending item categories in the far left "Item" column in the same order as shown on your spending plan form.

2) Every evening, record (in pencil) the cash you spent that day (cash only; checks written will be done later).

3) At the end of every month, review your check book and fill in what you spent on various days in the various spending categories.

4) Then, total the rows for each spending category and compare to what was budgeted; make adjustments on your spending plan for the future as needed.

ITEM	1	2	3	4	5	6	7	8	9	10	11	12	13	14	15	16	17	18	19	20	21	22	23	24	25	26	27	28	29	30	31	TOTALS
Gas		12		20						18				13					22													73
Eating Out							18			3			8				15				21											77
Newspprs																																
Snacks			2			2			2			4			5			2														17
Coffee	3		3	3				3	3	3			3	3		3			3		3											33

Special Order Form

Discover Learning, Inc. publishes several adult learning methodology self-study workbooks that are designed to build financial skills and increase employee understanding of financial concepts. The books are an excellent method of helping employees fully utilize their 401(k, 457 or defined benefit retirement plans. The books may be ordered directly using the following form.

TO: **DISCOVER LEARNING, INC.**
P.O. BOX 130857
ANN ARBOR, MI 48113-0857
Ph. (734) 669-8790
Fax (734) 669-8792
www.discover-learning.com

☐   **YES,** I would like to order at no risk* the following DLI books at prices shown, plus shipping and handling.**

Quantity	*Title*		*Amount*
_____	**CONTROLLING YOUR FINANCIAL FUTURE: HOW TO INCREASE YOUR WEALTH, DECREASE YOUR DEBT, AND MANAGE YOUR CASH FLOW™** (Basic financial planning in a self-study workbook format - 130 pages)	$19.95	_____
_____	**FINDING THE RIGHT FINANCIAL AND LEGAL ADVISORS FOR YOU™** (Self-study workbook format - 100 pages)	$19.95	_____
_____	**SECURING YOUR FINANCIAL FUTURE: HOW TO MAXIMIZE YOUR 457™** (Self-study *workbook* format - 90 pages)	$19.95	_____
_____	**SECURING YOUR FINANCIAL FUTURE: HOW TO MAXIMIZE YOUR 401(k)™** (Self-study *workbook* format - 90 pages)	$19.95	_____
_____	**SECURING YOUR FINANCIAL FUTURE: HOW TO MAXIMIZE YOUR 401(k)™** (*Recording of a four-hour workshop on audiotape or CDROM* format with self-study workbook and worksheets)	$59.95	_____
	Postage and handling**		_____
	Michigan Tax at 6%		_____
	TOTAL AMOUNT DUE WITH PLACEMENT OF ORDER	$	_____

Ship To:

_____

_____

Email address: _____

Please charge the following credit card: ☐ MasterCard ☐ Visa ☐ AMEX Exp. Date: _____

Account number: _____ Name as it appears on card: _____

Signature: _____

☐ Send Volume Purchase Discount Information

*No Risk: If for <u>any</u> reason, I am not completely satisfied, I understand the materials may be returned within 30 days for a full refund. **Add 5% postage to total order.